The DOUBLEDAY LARGE PRINT NEEDLECRAFT BOOK™

Mildred Graves Ryan

Photographs by R. B. Boris
Drawings by Marta Cone

GUILDAMERICA BOOKS™

Doubleday Direct, Inc., Garden City, New York

Published 1999 by GuildAmerica®Books,
an imprint of Doubleday Direct, Inc.,
Dept. GB, 401 Franklin Avenue,
Garden City, New York 11530

Exclusively available through
Doubleday Large Print™
America's only large-print book club.

GuildAmerica® Books is an imprint and registered
trademark and Doubleday Large Print™
is a trademark registration pending of
Doubleday Direct, Inc.

ISBN: 978-0-7394-0477-5

**This Large Print Book carries the
seal of approval of N.A.V.H.**

Contents

Preface

To use my hands to produce something attractive has always been a satisfying experience. It all began when I was four, when I wanted to imitate my mother and grandmothers, who sat down in the afternoon to do their "fancy work." My first piece of embroidery became part of a quilt which I am very proud to display today.

As the years passed I watched family members grow older, but always with their needlework. Eyes became clouded, hands gnarled and stiff, and stitches weren't quite as dainty, but always there was pride in their eyes when they showed me their latest bit of handiwork.

As I prepared this book, one thing was very much in my thoughts. What could I write about that would stimulate young and old alike with impaired vision to a greater enjoyment of needlecraft, to know the creative pleasure that comes from watching something lovely develop in the hands? What would readers want to make? How would they want to do it? What needles, yarns, tools, would be convenient for them to use?

With these questions in mind, I had some brainstorming sessions, browsed through boutiques, and checked the availability of supplies. In our get-togethers women of all ages discussed the pros and cons of needlework. Most of them wore glasses and many admitted to having cataracts.

In our round-table discussions we considered the types of yarn that were the easiest to handle, the ones they could distinguish through the sense of touch, helping them to work without mistakes. The women handled needles and hooks in different sizes and lengths. Not only was the ease of use considered but so was the comfort factor. How soon did eyes become teary, hands tired, shoulders aching?

We decided that color played a very important role. Dark colors were troublesome: stitches blended one into another, making it impossible to distinguish them. White was much preferred. Even the color of a hook or needle contributed to solving the visibility problem. A contrast in color was needed. For instance, working on canvas against a dark background makes it easier to see the holes.

As to projects, small, flat ones seemed easier to handle, with stitches easier to keep track of. Large pieces often required constant counting, and mistakes were more frequent. The quicker a project could be completed had its advantages. People became bored with lengthy undertakings.

Several of the women increased their incomes by selling their needlework. They wanted ideas. What could their eager fingers produce that would prove profitable? "Handmade" seems important to many customers.

Finding the desired supplies was a problem whether one lived in the city or the country. This caused the needleworker to be constantly substituting one material for another.

In discussing various types of handwork, it became apparent that everyone had her favorite. Some enjoyed crocheting; others hated it. Knitting was preferred by some. Then there were the advocates of quilting and embroidery, who delighted in watching a needle ply through the fabric with such happy results.

To answer these questions, this book has been written. It is divided into four sections: crocheting, knitting, quilting, and decorative stitching, which includes simple flat, cross, and needlepoint stitches. At the beginning of each part, some information is given to refresh your memory or provide step-by-step directions for someone who is just beginning to enjoy that form of needlecraft. And at the end there are instructions for items that you can make.

In doing the research, I discovered that while people made things for themselves, they like to construct something to give as a gift or to sell. With this in mind, I searched boutiques and specialty shops for the smart little article that would be interesting to make and at the same time fill a need, such as the double eyeglass case.

There has also been an attempt to spark your creative talents. Hints for substituting materials and colors to suit your taste are mentioned. Use the directions simply as a guide to produce other effects. Because it is often so difficult to find a specific type of yarn in a definite color, an attempt has been given to provide general guidelines throughout.

As always when preparing a book of this type, one relies on one's friends and associates for ideas and encouragement. I was very fortunate to have just such a group willing to share ideas and helpful information. Among them were Mary Faber, Fern Graves, Edna Jordon, Genevieve Perry, Eugenie Rives, Lonnie Sargent, and Sally Wellbery. Then there were Sally Signor, who sketched possible design patterns, and Evelyn Foster, who spent hours experimenting and then making many of the items shown in this book. I am indeed most grateful to them all. I am also indebted to the many people who supplied information concerning supplies and designs, and to those companies who granted permission to reproduce photographs and directions and especially to June King of Coats & Clark, Incorporated.

M.G.R.

PART I

Crocheting

Crocheting is a craft that allows for versatility. A simple stitch and a plain yarn can produce a wide variety of articles ranging from the practical to the frivolous. On the following pages you will find some suggestions for making the crocheting process easier to understand and more interesting to do.

The Beginning Steps

Preparing the yarn carefully and learning to manipulate your fingers so the yarn and hook move in perfect coordination are important.

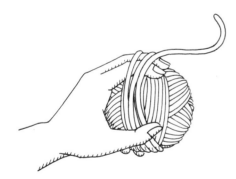

Wind the Yarn. Sometimes no preparation is necessary, for the yarn is already wound in a ball, but if it isn't, then it is best to wind it into one. There are various ways to do this, but this seems the easiest. Begin by wrapping yarn loosely around your fingers. Remove loops and place in your left hand in line with your fingers. This allows you to cross loops as you continue to wind yarn around your fingers. From time to time, slip your fingers from under loops and turn ball. Keeping your fingers under the loops prevents the yarn from being stretched.

Hold the Hook. Although both hands are needed to hold yarn and hook, most people find it more natural to hold the hook in the right hand. Because of this, directions are written for the right-handed person.

To grasp hook as a pencil, place it in your right hand between thumb and first finger with hook downward. Put middle finger near end of hook and thumb and first finger closer to center.

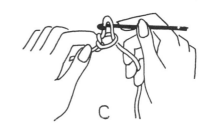

Make a Slip Knot. Crocheting begins with a slip loop or knot. Pick up yarn about 2 inches from end. Hold it between your thumb and first finger, twisting it into a small circle. Let the strand fall in back of circle (A). Pass hook through circle (B). Pick up yarn and pull a small loop through it (C), making a slip knot.

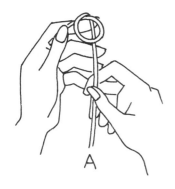

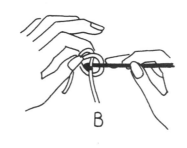

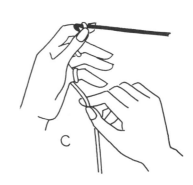

Hold the Yarn. Place yarn in left hand. Run ball end through your fingers about 4 inches from loop (A). Keep palm up and wrap yarn around the base of the little finger, bringing it under back of the ring finger, over the middle one, and under the first finger (B). You may need to adjust yarn so you can hold loop between thumb and first finger. Pull yarn down gently so it lies firmly, but not tightly (C). This allows you to regulate the flow of the yarn.

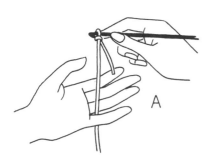

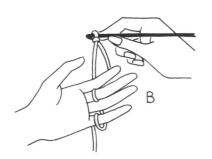

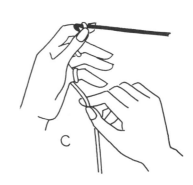

The Basic Stitches

Chain Stitch. This stitch forms the foundation for other stitches. It is an easy stitch to make but requires care so size of chain and tension are even. The stitch should be loose enough to allow hook to pass through it, but not so tight that the edge curls up.

Start with a slip knot. Move hook through loop from right to left. Pull end of yarn until loop clings to hook.

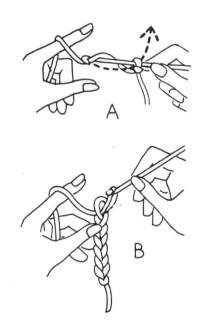

Hold yarn in left hand, as well as slip knot, between thumb and first finger. Keep yarn taut over first finger, which is bent slightly as you pass hook through loop from right to left, under and over yarn. The yarn seems to wrap the hook, and at the same time the hook catches the yarn (A). Pull yarn through loop, making first chain. Repeat this process as many times as necessary (B). Try to keep thumb and first finger close to stitch being made.

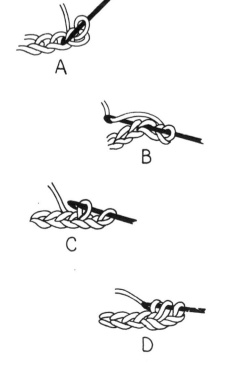

Single Crochet. This stitch is the narrowest of the basic stitches. It creates a flat, firm texture, whether you are working on the straight or in the round. The stitch can also be used to finish an article and to join parts of a design together.

For a straight row of single crochet stitches, start with a chain the required length. Hold chain with right side toward you. Place hook in second chain from end, inserting it from front of stitch to back (A).

Move hook under and over yarn. Catch yarn and pull it through chain stitch (B). Notice that you now have 2 loops on hook (C).

Put yarn over hook again. Pull it through 2

loops (D), leaving 1 loop on hook (E). A single crochet stitch has been made.

To make the *second single crochet,* insert the hook in the next chain stitch and follow steps above. Proceed in this way until a single crochet is made in each of the chain stitches.

Crochet 1 chain stitch to end the row (F). Turn the work so the reverse side is toward you (G).

To make *next row* of single crochet, put hook in second stitch from hook, which is the last stitch of preceding row. Slip hook from front to back under the 2 top threads (H). Pull through yarn to make a single crochet stitch. Continue in this manner until row is finished.

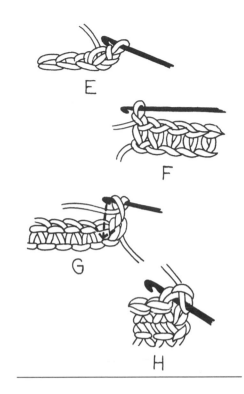

When making *single crochet stitches in the round,* start with a short foundation chain, which will become center of circle. Join first and last stitches by passing hook through the loop of the first chain, to form ring or circle. Crochet from right side. Put yarn over hook and draw through the 2 loops on hook (A). One loop remains on hook (B). The ring has been made.

For *first round,* make 8 single crochet stitches through center of ring (C).

Before beginning second round, indicate end of first round with a marker or small safety pin (D). Always move marker at end of each row. To make *second round,* take 2 single crochets into each stitch of the previous round. When round is completed, there will be 16 stitches on the hook.

For the *third round,* make a single crochet in first stitch and 2 single crochets in the next stitch. Continue this way so there is an increase of 1 stitch in every other stitch in this row. This leaves 24 stitches on round (E). Continue

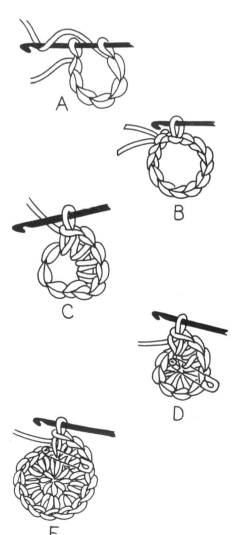

crocheting until desired number of rounds are made. One increases 1 stitch every other stitch.

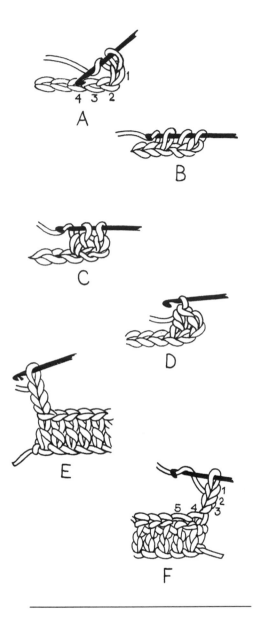

Double Crochet. Begin with a foundation chain, using an even number of stitches. Start first row by placing yarn over hook. Put hook in fourth chain from hook, passing it under the 2 top threads (A). Draw it through chain. Three loops remain on hook. Then place yarn over hook (B) and draw through the first 2 loops.

Put yarn over the hook again (C) and draw it through remaining 2 loops. This leaves 1 loop on the hook (D) and completes a double crochet stitch.

To make the *second double crochet,* put yarn over hook. Insert hook from the front in next chain stitch, slipping it under the 2 top threads. Continue as you did for the first double crochet. At end of row, make 3 chain stitches (E). Turn crocheting so reverse side is toward you.

For *second row,* put yarn over hook. Place hook in fifth stitch from hook, moving it under the 2 top strands (F). Continue as you did for first row.

Half Double Crochet. As you may imagine, this stitch falls between single and double crochet in size. It produces a firm material with a ridged textural effect. Start with a chain the required length. To begin first stitch, put yarn over hook. Insert it in third chain from hook. Be sure to enter from front and pass under the 2 top threads (A).

Draw yarn through stitch, leaving 3 loops on hook (B).

Put yarn over hook. Bring it through all loops

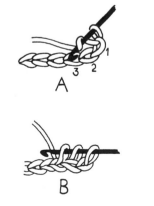

6

on hook (C). One loop remains on hook (D). You have made a half double crochet. For *next half double crochet,* place yarn over hook. Insert hook in next chain. Remember to enter from front under the 2 top strands. Proceed as for first stitch.

When you have completed the row, chain 2 stitches (E) and turn the piece. The turning chain-2 does not count as a stitch on next row.

To make *second row,* place yarn over hook. Insert hook in first stitch, which is last stitch of previous row. Work from front under the 2 top loops. Continue to make half double crochet stitches as you did for preceding row.

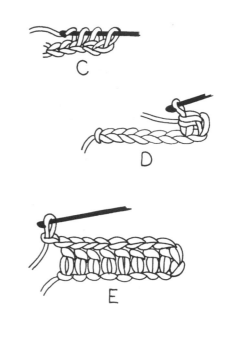

Treble or Triple Crochet. This stitch provides a more open texture with rows farther apart. Begin with a foundation chain the required length. For first treble, put yarn over hook twice (A). Insert hook in fifth chain from hook. Enter from front under the 2 top threads. Put yarn over hook and bring through chain stitch. Four loops are left on hook (B). Put yarn over hook again and pull through 2 loops (C), leaving 3 loops on hook. Place yarn over hook again and draw through 2 loops (D). Two loops remain on the hook.

Wrap yarn over again and draw through 2 loops (E). Now only 1 loop remains on hook. The first treble stitch has been made (F).

To make *second stitch,* put yarn over hook twice. Insert hook under the 2 top threads of next stitch. Proceed as for first treble stitch.

Complete row by making a treble stitch in each chain. Chain 4 stitches. They will become first treble on second row.

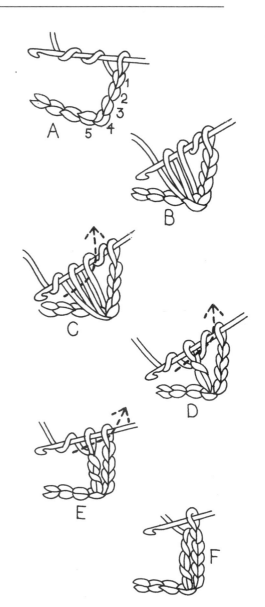

Turn work to begin *second row.* Put yarn over hook twice. Insert hook in sixth stitch from hook. Enter from front under 2 top threads. This stitch falls in line with second stitch on preceding row. Continue to work as for first row (G).

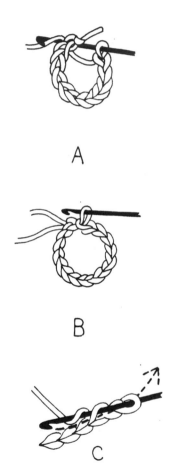

A

B

C

Slip Stitch. This stitch has an important place in crocheting, although it isn't thought of as actually constructing anything. Instead, it is used as a joining or an invisible stitch when making a ring or a round medallion, crocheting 2 finished edges together, or as an edging to give firmness.

To *close a chain* in order to make a ring, put hook in stitch at end of chain to be joined (A). Put yarn over hook. Pull it through stitch and loop on hook. This movement closes ring and leaves 1 loop on hook (B).

Sometimes a slip stitch is used in *a row* of stitches. It can even be employed for a complete row. For this, insert hook in the second stitch from hook. Put yarn over hook (C). Draw it through stitch and loop on hook. To crochet another slip stitch, put hook in the next stitch and continue the procedure (D).

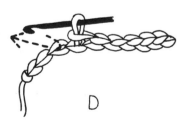

D

Afghan Stitch. This stitch creates an entirely different look in crocheting. It has a definite textural quality that seems to look like knitting more than crocheting.

The afghan stitch is made with a special long hook that resembles a knitting needle with a hook replacing the point. As the work proceeds from right to left across a row, each stitch remains on the hook, but as the crocheting moves from left to right, the stitches are removed from the hook. But you must remember not to turn your work as you do for regular crocheting—to make the afghan stitch you always work on the same side. Notice, though, how different the 2 sides look.

Start with a row of chain stitches the required length.

For the *first row*, insert hook in second chain from hook. Put yarn over hook and draw a loop through stitch. Work this way to end of row, leaving all loops on hook (A).

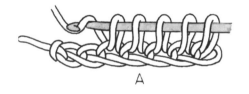

For the *second row*, remove loops from hook in same way without turning piece. Put yarn over hook. Pull a loop through first stitch on hook. Then put yarn over hook and pull it through 2 loops (B). Repeat this process to end of row. At end of row, make 1 chain.

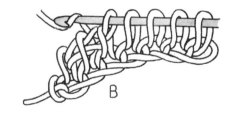

For the *third row*, work from right to left, leaving loops on hook as for first row. Insert hook under vertical stitch. Place yarn over hook and draw through a loop. Continue working this way to end of row.

For the *fourth row*, crochet the way you did for second row.

To continue the crocheting, repeat third and fourth rows.

9

Understanding the Directions

Instructions for making an article are usually written in an abbreviated language. At first glance, they often seem puzzling and difficult to understand and remember. If you have had that experience, you will find the reference list given here helpful.

Abbreviations. The ones listed here are used in this book or are found quite often in books or patterns.

beg	beginning		RH	right-hand
ch st	chain stitch		rnd	round
dec	decrease		R	row
dc	double crochet		sc	single crochet
hdc, h dc	half double crochet		sk	skip
			sl st	slip stitch
hk	hook		sp	space
incl	inclusive		st	stitch
inc	increase		sts	stitches
K	knit		tog	together
LH	left-hand		tr	treble or triple crochet
lp	loop			
pat, patt	pattern		tch	turning chain
P	purl		yo	yarn over or around hook
rep, * *, ** **	repeat			

Single (* *), double (** **), and triple (*** ***) pairs of asterisks are sometimes found, indicating that a series of procedures is to be repeated. For instance, if you see directions such as "*3 dc in next st, 1 dc in following st, repeat from * twice," you know that instructions between the asterisks should be repeated twice.

Sometimes parentheses ( ) and brackets [ ] are used to indicate a repetition. They can also be employed to set apart a sequence of stitches to be placed in a stitch or space.

Special Terms. Sometimes directions do not give a complete explanation of how something should be done. In order to prevent any misunderstanding, a more complete explanation is offered here for certain terms.

Attaching yarn when you have nearly used up the yarn you are working with: try to crochet up to the last step of the stitch you are making, and then pick up the new yarn and pull it through the stitch, completing the last step (A). Cut the original yarn to about 2 inches. Turn the piece. Place ends of the 2 threads over previous row. Crochet over them for about 4 stitches (B). Try to avoid using a knot.

A *new color* can be introduced at the beginning of a row. Put yarn over last few stitches of row below. Continue to crochet with the first color, covering end of new yarn. Work with first color to last 2 loops of final stitch. Then draw new color through these 2 loops (C).

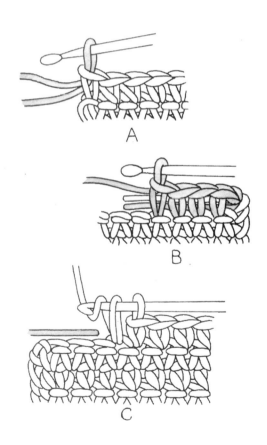

A

B

C

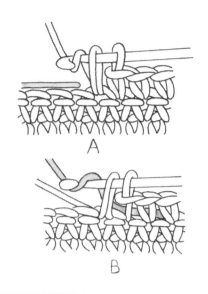

Attaching the yarn mid-row is sometimes necessary, especially when introducing a new color. Place yarn over previous row, starting a few stitches before it is needed (A). Continue to crochet with original yarn, covering end of new yarn. Work with first color to last 2 loops of final stitch. Then draw new color through these 2 loops (B).

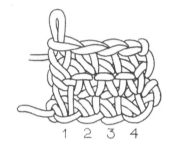

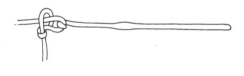

Counting stitches isn't always easy. Studying the drawing shown here may prove helpful.

Draw through means to pull the yarn, which has been placed over the hook, through stitch or loop.

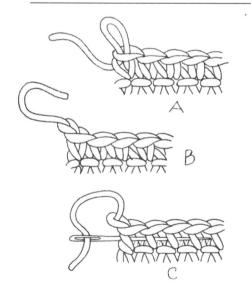

End off indicates that it is time to stop and fasten the yarn. Do this by cutting yarn about 3 inches from last stitch. Put hook in last loop. Place yarn over hook. Draw it completely through loop (A). Pull yarn to tighten stitch (B). To hide the end, thread a needle with yarn. Weave it through the back below the top row of stitches (C).

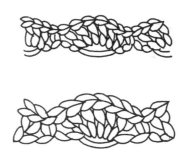

Gauge is too important to be overlooked. When it is disregarded, the work may be larger or smaller than it should be. "Gauge" refers to the number of stitches and rows needed to produce a piece of crocheting of a certain size when a certain needle and yarn is used. Usually the gauge is listed at the beginning of the directions —so many stitches to an inch.

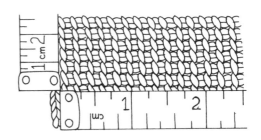

Making a test piece before you begin to crochet is a good idea. If the number of the stitches and rows is not the same, you should make some changes. Changing the hook is one way to do this. If the number of stitches is fewer than the number required, use a smaller hook; use a larger one when there are more than the necessary number.

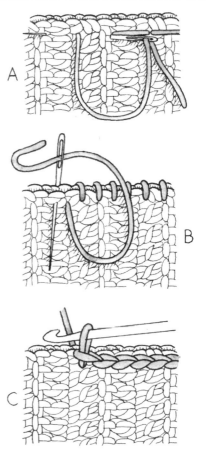

Joining the crocheted pieces can be done in a number of ways. The method you select depends on the edge and effect you wish. Usually an invisible seam as the best choice. Although the seam should be strong, it should be elastic enough to retain the elasticity of the crocheting. The seaming can be done by sewing or crocheting. For a *sewn seam* you can use a backstitch or an overhand stitch. For the *backstitch seam* (A), place row of backstitches close to the edges, using matching yarn. Be careful not to pull the stitches tight. An *overhand joining* allows the seam to open up for a flat finish (B). The stitches are taken over the edges. Keep the stitches even.

For a *crocheted joining,* place the right sides of 2 pieces together. Pull up a loop through a corresponding stitch, 1 in each piece (C). Then pass the hook through the next 2 stitches. Draw up a loop through both stitches and the one on the hook. Work this way until the seam is completed. A chainlike effect appears along the seam line.

Shaping. By decreasing and increasing the number of stitches the size and shape of a piece of crocheting can be altered. The changes can be made at the ends of a row or somewhere between. The directions will indicate where the decrease or increase is to be made.

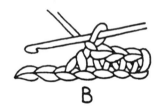

To decrease in single crochet, work until 2 loops are left on hook. Insert hook in next stitch. Place yarn over hook. Draw it through stitch, leaving 3 loops on hook. Put yarn over hook again (A) and draw it through the 3 loops, leaving 1 loop on hook (B). This method can also be used for half double crochet.

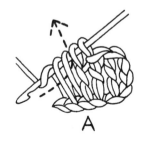

To decrease in double crochet, construct a double crochet to place where 2 loops remain on hook. Put yarn over hook. Insert hook in the next stitch and draw a loop through the stitch. Four loops remain on hook. Put yarn over hook (A). Pull it through 2 loops, leaving 3 on hook. Put yarn over hook again (B). Draw it through the 3 loops, leaving 1 loop on hook (C).

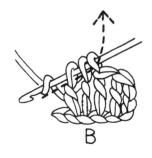

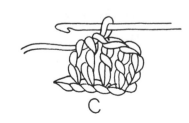

To decrease in afghan stitch, insert the hook under 2 vertical bars. Draw up 1 loop. When crocheting at the *right end,* join the first and second stitches by drawing up a loop in second bar and bring this loop through the first (A). A decrease at the *left end* of the work is made on the return row. Place the yarn over the hook. Pull a loop through 2 loops, instead of the usual 1, to make the first stitch (B).

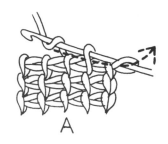

A

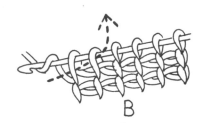

B

To increase a stitch, make 2 stitches in 1 stitch instead of only 1. The procedure can be used for the various types of crochet stitches (A).

To increase 2 stitches, crochet 3 stitches in a single stitch instead of only 1 stitch. This technique can also be used for the various types of stitches (B).

To increase the number of stitches at the end of a row, chain the required number of stitches extending beyond the edge. Turn the work. Crochet along the chain on the next row (C).

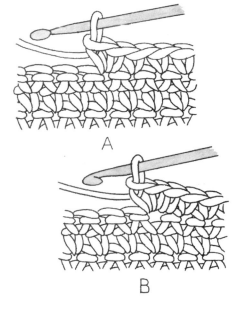

A

B

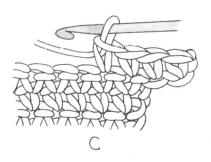

C

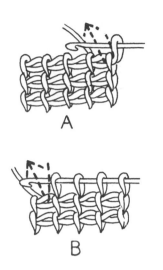

A

B

To increase when working afghan stitches, add a stitch by pulling up a loop in the chain stitch between the vertical bars. This is done on the row in which loops are made and kept on the hook.

If the increase is to be made at the beginning of a row, make a loop in the first vertical bar (A). At the opposite end, work a loop between the last 2 vertical bars, entering the top part of the chain. Then pull up a loop in the last vertical bar (B).

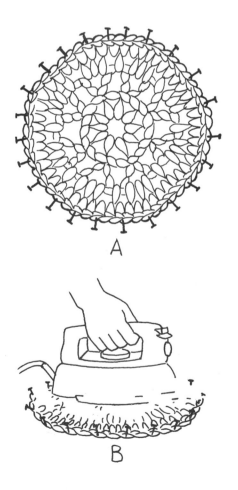

A

B

Blocking shapes a crochet article, giving it a more finished look. Smooth the piece out on a well-padded board. The wrong side should be up. Pin it with rustproof pins, first at the top and bottom and then at the sides. Gently stretch and shape the pieces to the required measurements. Place the pins close together to avoid a scalloped edge (A). Articles made with synthetic yarns can be dampened and allowed to dry. Pressing with an iron is not necessary. When working with some smooth yarns in flat rows, it is possible to cover the article with a damp cloth. Press lightly, allowing the steam to penetrate the article (B). Do not slide the iron or let it rest on the crocheting. Let the piece remain on the board until thoroughly dry.

Turning Work. In order for the rows to remain straight, a turning chain is used. The number of chains varies depending on the type of stitch being used. For single crochet, use 1 chain; half double crochet, 2 chains; double crochet, 3 chains; treble crochet, 4 chains.

Under Two Top Threads. This direction is frequently used. The hook is slipped under the top part of the stitch.

Work Even. This term means to continue to work the stitch pattern using the same number of stitches without any increases or decreases.

Yarn Over. The hook is maneuvered passing under the yarn so the hook catches it in preparation for drawing it through a loop or stitch.

Some Tools to Consider

A hook and some yarn are all you really need to crochet. However, you may find that a few small pieces of equipment make it easier for you to work more efficiently.

Tools. Hooks are made in a variety of materials, lengths, and sizes and in two types—regular and afghan. Fortunately, the directions you use usually list the size of the hook you will need. This information is a great help because the yarn and the hook are dependent on each other. It is impossible to create the right effect if they are not compatible. In choosing a hook, check it carefully. It should be nicely shaped and cut deeply enough so that it can hold the yarn securely as the stitch is being crocheted. You also want one that is lightweight and comfortable to hold, so you can control it easily.

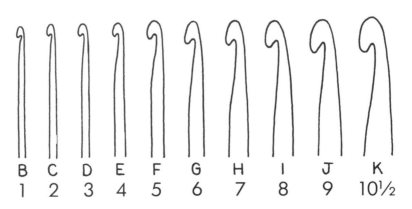

B	C	D	E	F	G	H	I	J	K
1	2	3	4	5	6	7	8	9	10½

Among the small gadgets there is a *counter*. With it you can count stitches and rows. Then there is a *gauge* for checking hook sizes, and *markers* with an open coil ring for indicating a special feature. Then there are some sewing aids to be considered. A *needle* with a large eye such as a tapestry needle, a *needle threader, scissors, ruler,* and *tape measure* should be kept handy. And of course you should have something to hold your equipment. A bag is probably the easiest to carry, but be sure to keep the hooks protected and the small gadgets separated so they will be easy to locate in the bag. One you might like to make is shown on page 40.

Yarn. Of course, the results are best when you use the yarn that is suggested in the directions for the article you are crocheting. There may be, however, occasions when it is impossible to locate a particular yarn. At such times, it is helpful to have some knowledge about various yarns so you can make a good substitution. Train your fingers to analyze certain characteristics by touch. Keep a file of crochet samples. Pin a sample to the label. In this way, you will know how the yarn behaves and the effect it creates.

Usually the label that bands a ball or skein of yarn provides a wealth of information. The fiber content, the ply, the weight, and care instructions are usually listed, as well as other pertinent information.

Cotton has become more popular as a yarn in recent years. The yarn is soft and less elastic than wool. It is made in various weights, and frequently as a cord.

Synthetics, as a group, continue to grow. In fact, it is often hard to find anything but this type of yarn, and in this grouping there are variations. The decided advantage of synthetic yarn is the ability to be washed and dried by machine.

Wool has many outstanding characteristics. It has a lovely softness, but at the same time it is strong and elastic, making it durable and long-wearing.

Generally the label mentions *ply*. This term refers to the number of threads that are twisted together to make a strand of yarn and not to weight.

The mention of weight in relation to yarn may seem confusing. You may find the actual weight listed as well as terms such as "lightweight" and "sportsweight." In the first case the number denotes the actual weight of the ball, whereas in the second it describes the thickness of the yarn.

Choosing Something to Make

Although it is exciting to choose a project, it isn't always easy to find just the right one. Too often one thinks only of the beauty of the item, and not of one's personal capabilities. On the next few pages you will find some suggestions, with instructions. Each project has been chosen because it is simple to crochet and easy to handle. Starting with something simple and progressing to the more difficult is the best route to take.

Pictorial Blanket

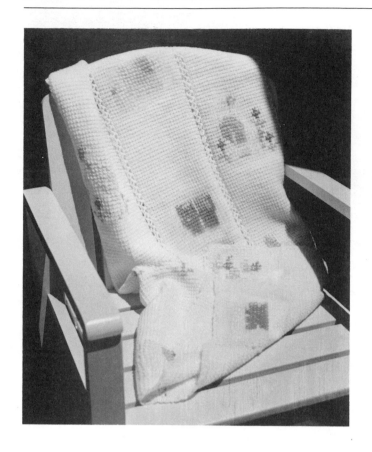

Embroidery and lacy edging give this simple afghan a bright, dainty look. Worked in panels for easy handling, the afghan stitches make a perfect background for the capering animals. Although the design shown here is for the baby, it could be crocheted in a darker color and floral designs for an adult lap robe with a Victorian flavor.

Information to Note

Size: Afghan approximately 34 × 42 inches
Each panel approximately 6½ × 42 inches

Material: 6 skeins white 2-ply baby yarn
For embroidery, 1 skein 2-ply baby yarn in each of 4 colors —pink, yellow, blue, green and a small amount of black

Tools: Afghan hook—Size 10
Crochet hook—Size 6
Tapestry needle

Gauge: 5 st = 1 inch

Directions to Follow

The afghan is easier to make if you crochet each panel and then embroider them and finally put them together.

Panels: Start by chaining 28 stitches, using an afghan hook. Work loosely.
Row 1: Insert hook in 2nd ch from the hook. Be careful not to twist chain. Put yo hook and draw a lp through the ch st. Continue this way to end of row, leaving all lps on the hook.

Row 2: Do not turn work. Place yo hook. Draw a lp through the 1st st on hook. Then rep the following procedure until only 1 ch remains on the hook. Put yo hook and draw it through next 2 lps.

Row 3: Counting lp on hook as 1st lp of row, insert hook under 2nd vertical bar. Put yo and draw up a lp. Rep this procedure across row, leaving all sts on hook. You should have 28 lps on hook.

Row 4: Repeat row 2, removing lps from hook.

Continue crocheting rows 2 and 3 until panel measures 42 inches. Fasten yarn. Mark the lower edge. This makes it easier to join the panels so all stitches are running in the same direction.

Edging for Panel. Use a No. 6 crochet hook. Start with a sl st in the lower corner of the panel. Then, working along the long edge, ch 4, sk 2 rows, sc in next row. Continue *ch 4, sk 1 row, sc in next row. Rep from * around 4 sides of panel.

Embroidery. One cross is made over 1 afghan stitch. The accompanying chart offers a suggested layout for the placement of the designs. Measure

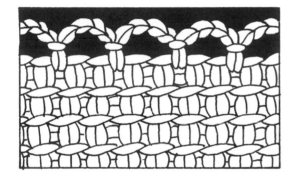

Kitten		Rabbit		Elephant
	Bear		Duck	
Lamb		Kitten		Lamb
	Rabbit		Rabbit	
Bear		Elephant		Duck
	Duck		Bear	
Elephant		Lamb		Kitten

carefully so overall look will appear balanced. Be sure that all of the designs are running in the same direction.

Try to keep the work from stretching as you do the embroidery. Begin by weaving colored yarn through afghan stitches for about 1 inch on wrong side. A length of yarn about 18 inches is easiest to work with. Bring yarn to right side. Work from left to right, making a row of slanting stitches. To complete the stitches, work from right to left, crossing the 1st row of slanting stitches. Repeat this procedure until design is embroidered. Fasten the yarn by weaving it through the stitches on the wrong side for about 1 inch. Do this carefully so the back of the afghan looks neat, without any dangling ends.

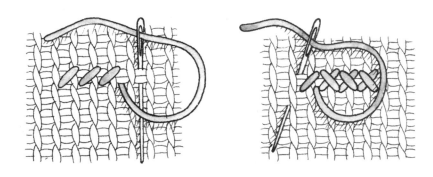

Joining Panels. Work with the first 2 panels. Attach yarn at lower edge of 1st panel. Then ch 4, sc in corner of 2nd panel. Continue this way: *ch 2, sc in lp of 1st panel, ch 2, sc in lp of 2nd panel.* End with ch 2, sc in corner of panel, ch 4, sc in corner of next panel. Fasten yarn. Proceed to join all panels in the same way.

Border Edging. Work around the 4 sides this way, using crochet hook.

Row 1: Attach yarn in 1st sp at lower edge. Then repeat this procedure: *ch 4, sc in next sp.*

Row 2: Rep Row 1.

Row 3: Crochet 4 sc in each sp around 4 sides of afghan. Fasten yarn.

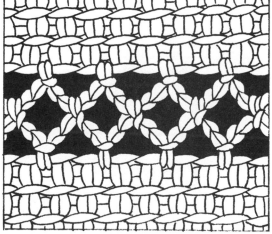

✕ BLUE
⭘ PINK
• YELLOW
◺ GREEN
▼ BLACK

23

The Versatile Ball

"Pretty, pliable, and practical" seems to describe this ball of many uses—a toy for the baby, a scented accessory for the closet, an ornament for the Christmas tree, or an exercise gadget for a weakened wrist. Specially made single crochet stitches and a rainbow of colors add interest, as does a bit of sachet or potpourri tucked inside.

DARK OLIVE GREEN
PALE BLUE
GRAY
BRIGHT GREEN
LAVENDER
DARK OLIVE GREEN
DARK OLIVE GREEN
ROSY RED
MEDIUM BLUE
BRIGHT GREEN
PINK
DARK OLIVE GREEN
DARK OLIVE GREEN
ROSY RED
PALE MUSTARD YELLOW
BRIGHT GREEN
PEACH
DARK OLIVE GREEN

Information to Note

Size: Circumference 12 inches
Materials: For each stripe, 2½ yards of 4-ply yarn; a suggested color arrangement is shown here
Cotton batting; sachet or potpourri
Tools: Crochet hook—Size **J**
Tapestry needle
Gauge: 4 st = 1 inch

Directions to Follow

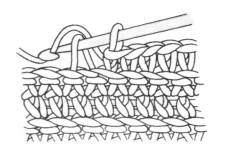

NOTE: All sc sts are worked in back lp.

Making Stripes: Begin by chaining 19 sts.

Row 1: Make a sc in 2nd ch from hook. Continue with a sc in each ch. At end of row, ch 1 and turn.

Row 2: Put a sl st in the 1st 4 sc sts. Then continue with a sc in each sc. When row is completed, ch 1 and turn.

Row 3: Rep row 2, completing the 1st stripe or ridge. Fasten and clip yarn.

Remaining Stripes: Rep rows 2 and 3, attaching yarn in a contrasting color before starting another row. Continue until there are 18 stripes.

Finishing: Sew sides together. Gather stripes together to close one end. Fill the covering with cotton batting. Tuck in a bit of sachet if you wish. Fold in the ends of yarn at the other end. Gather stripes together. Fasten yarn. If you plan to hang the ball, leave a length of yarn from which you can make a chained loop.

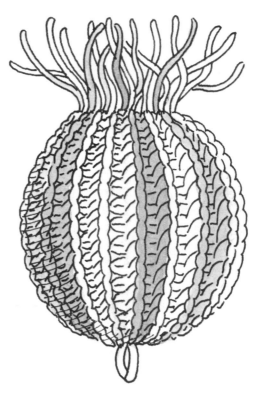

Lap Robe with Pinwheels

Using a favorite patchwork design adds a lively feeling to this coverlet. Triangles making squares in two colors produces the pinwheel effect. Made of single crochet stitches, the crocheting follows a diagonal line, giving an interesting textural quality to the squares.

Information to Note

Size: Lap robe approximately 38 × 54 inches

Materials: 6 skeins red (A) 3-ply Coats & Clark Red Heart® yarn
5 skeins white (B) 3-ply Coats & Clark Red Heart® yarn

Tools: Crochet Hook—Size G Tapestry needle

Gauge: 4 sc = 1 inch

Directions to Follow

SQUARE CONSTRUCTION

First Triangular Half: Ch 31 sts, using color A.

Row 1: Sc in 2nd ch from hook. Continue across row with a sc in each ch —30 sc. Check gauge. Work should measure about 8½ inches. Ch 1 loosely and turn.

Row 2: To start the dec to shape the square, sk 1st st, sc in each sc across to last 2 sts. Then sk 1st st before making sc in last stitch—28 sc. Ch 1 loosely. Turn.

Rows 3–15: Repeat row 2 until 2 sc remain. Ch 1 and turn.
Last row: Sk 1st sc, sc in last sc. Fasten yarn.

Second Triangular Half: Begin at the spot where you started the 1st half. Work on the right side of the triangle and along other side of starting chain.

Row 1: With 2nd color (B), make lp on hook. Sc in each of the 30 chs you started with. Crochet as you did for 1st triangular half.

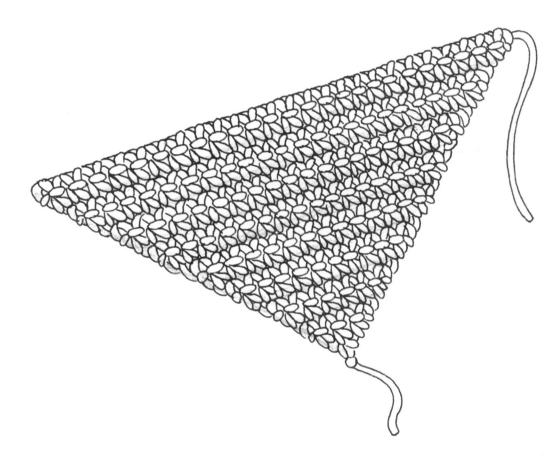

ASSEMBLE SQUARES

When you have made 54 squares, steam-press each lightly. The measurements should be identical for all squares. Arrange the smaller squares into a larger one, using the pattern shown here. Sew the small squares together. Then sew the pinwheel squares together to form the lap robe. Weave the ends of yarn into the crocheting on the wrong side to secure them. Clip the yarn close to the surface so there are no dangling threads.

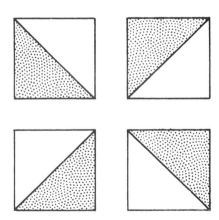

27

Edging: Finish the lap robe with a simple edging. A row of single crochet stitches will create a firm edge with a chain-stitch finish.

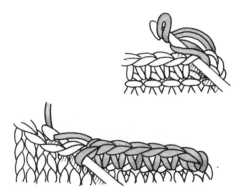

Work with the right side toward you. Insert the hook near the right-hand corner. Place the yarn around the hook and draw it through to the right side. Hold both ends of the yarn together at the back as you insert the hook into the next stitch. Put both ends of yarn around the hook and draw through loop. This procedure secures the yarn. Complete the single crochet in the usual way. Continue across the edge, making a simple crochet in each stitch. To turn a corner, work 2 or 3 stitches into the corner stitch. Be sure to keep the edge flat. The stitches should not be pulled together, which would create a curled effect. If you wish, a wider border can be crocheted.

Jaunty Knob "Hat"

Touching a hot knob on a pot lid is a most unpleasant experience! To avoid a catastrophe, use one of these little holders. It fits over the knob easily and provides the needed protection.

Information to Note

Size: Approximately 3 inches
Materials: Bits of 4-ply yarn in 1 or 2 colors
Tool: Crochet hook—Size H
Gauge: 5 dc = 1 inch

Directions to Follow

Begin by chaining 4 sts. Join with a sl st to form ring.

Rnd 1: Ch 3 sts. Crochet 8 dc in the ring. Make a sl st in lp of 1st dc.

Rnd 2: Ch 3 sts. Make 1 dc in 1st dc of previous row, counting the ch as a dc. Take 2 dc through both lps of each dc. Sl st in lp of 1st dc of rnd.

Rnd 3: Ch 3 sts. Dc in next st. Increase a dc in every other st of previous rnd. Join with a sl st. Fasten yarn and turn up this row, creating a hatlike look to the holder.

For a bow at the peak, cut a length of yarn the correct length. Pull it through the tip of the holder and tie a bow. A contrasting color usually makes it look cuter.

The Surprising Potholder

The most amazing thing happens as you crochet this potholder. As if by magic, two edges curl up without your help. And as this is happening, diagonal ridges appear that move differently on the upper and lower sides. By the addition of color to the design, a simple potholder takes on a dramatic look.

Information to Note

Size: Approximately 6 inches square

Materials: 1 skein of each of 2 colors in a 2-ply Coats & Clark Red Heart® sports yarn (scraps of yarn can be used) 1 small ring

Tools: Crochet hook—Size H Tapestry needle

Gauge: 5 sc = 1 inch

Directions to Follow

Begin by making a ch of 37 sts, using the paler yarn (A).

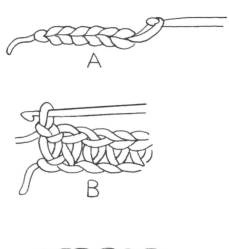

Using the ch as a foundation, continue to crochet around the ch, placing a sc in each ch on both sides (B). Be sure not to add or subtract a stitch as you continue round and round. Always keep sts even (C).

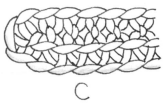

Continue to crochet in this way for 8 rnds. Then change color. No doubt by the time you make the color change you will notice that the edges are beginning to curl up.

When you have completed another 8 rnds, the edges will have come together, forming a diagonal pattern. Put the holder on a table and pull it gently into a square with the open edges, forming a diagonal at the center (D). Fasten the yarn, leaving an end long enough to sew the edges together and to attach a small ring or to crochet a loop.

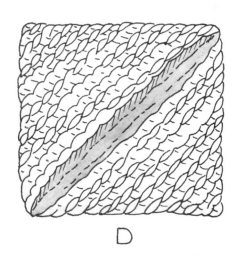

Place Mat in the Round

Curving doilies add a special decorative touch to a table setting. Crocheting them in alternating rows of the basic stitches creates an interesting textured design.

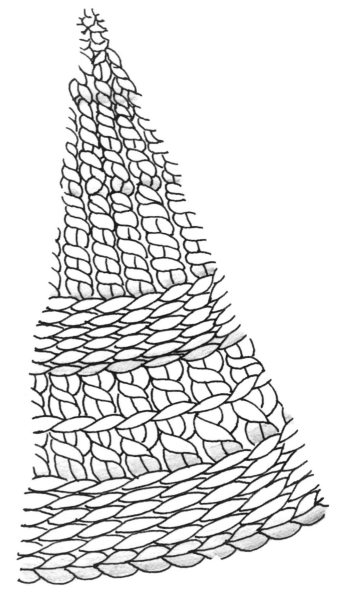

Information to Note

Size: Diameter 16 inches; because of the arrangement of the design pattern, it is possible to increase or decrease its size to fit your requirements

Material: 4 skeins soft 3-ply rug-weight yarn

Tool: Crochet hook—Size G

Gauge: 4 sts = 1 inch

Directions to Follow

Start with 6 ch sts. Join with sl st.

Rnd 1: Make a rnd of sc sts, putting 2 sts in each ch st (12 sts).

Rnd 2: Ch 2 sts. They are counted as 1 dc and mark the beg of the 2nd rnd. Rnd of dc sts, putting 2 sts in each sc st (24 sts).

Rnd 3: Ch 3 sts (counts as 1 tr st). Row of tr sts, placing 2 sts in each dc st (48 sts).

Rnd 4: Ch 3 sts. Another row of tr sts, placing 2 sts in each tr st (96 sts).

In crocheting the doily, watch the tension of your stitches. Work them loosely enough so it lies flat. From time to time, place it on a table and smooth it out. If the edge has a tendency to curl up, you know that you are crocheting too tightly or you are not remembering to make the necessary increases.

Rnd 5: Make a row of sl sts, adding 1 st at every 5th st.

Rnd 6: Row of sl sts, adding 1 st at every 6th st.

Rnd 7: Row of sl sts, adding 1 st at every 7th st.

Rnd 8: Row of sl sts, adding 1 st at every 8th st.

Rnd 9: Row of sl sts, adding 1 st at every 9th st.

Rnd 10: Ch 2 sts. Make row of dc, increasing every 10th st.

Rnd 11: Crochet row of dc in back of every top st.

Rnds 12–16: Repeat rnds 5–9.

Rnd 17: Repeat rnd 10.

Rnd 18: Repeat rnd 11.

Rnds 19–23: Repeat rnds 5–9, ending with a rnd of sl sts.

Patchwork Rug

It may seem strange to find a popular quilt design on the floor. The geometric pattern of this log cabin design, however, seems right beside a bed or in front of a fireplace or a favorite chair. By working it in small pieces, you will find the construction easy to handle.

Information to Note

Size: Rug approximately 29 × 44 inches

Materials: Rug yarn in 5 different colors: For center squares, 2 skeins off-white (A) For rectangles, 4 skeins cocoa brown (B)
4 skeins olive green (C)
4 skeins dark green (D)
4 skeins chocolate brown (E)

Tool: Crochet hook—Size K

Gauge: 3 sc = 2 inches

Directions to Follow

Basic Construction: The rug is made of 6 patchwork squares, each of which is composed of 1 small square and 4 rectangular pieces. A different color is used for each of the pieces.

Small Square: Start with 11 ch sts.
Row 1: Sc in 2nd ch from hook. Continue with a sc in each ch (10 sc). Ch 1 and turn.

Rows 2–12: Sc in each sc. Ch 1 and turn at end of each row. Fasten yarn at end of row 12. Make 6.

Rectangles: Begin with 21 chs.

Row 1: Sc in 2nd ch from hook. Continue with a sc in each ch (20 sc). Ch 1 and turn.

Rows 2–12: Sc in each sc. Ch 1 and turn at end of each row. Fasten yarn at the end of row 12. Make 6 of each color.

Assemble a Square: Begin by attaching rectangle B to square A, then C to A and B, followed by D to A and C, and finally E to A, D, and B. This can be done with a sl st or with overhand sts. You can decide which method is easier to do and at the same time produces a firm, flat finish.

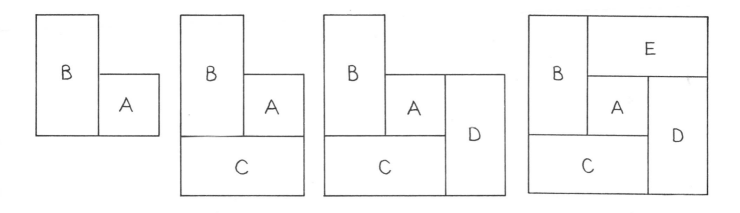

Join Squares: Put squares together so that each lies in the same pattern position. Work as you did in assembling each square. Placing the rug on a table will make it less cumbersome to handle (C).

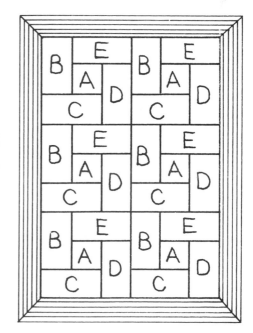

35

Border: To finish the rug, use a border of sc sts. Start by crocheting 1 rnd of sl sts around rug, working 1 sl st in each st and row, using yarn A. Crochet loosely enough so rug does not roll up.

Rnd 1: With yarn C, sc in back lp of each st around the rug. Work 3 sc in each corner. Use a sl st in 1st sc to join each rnd. Ch 1.

Rnd 2: Continue with yarn C. Make sc in each sc, putting 3 sc in each corner st.

Rnd 3: With yarn D, repeat rnd 2.

Rnd 4: Repeat rnd 2, using yarn D.

Rnds 5–6: Repeat rnd 2, using yarn B.

Rnds 7–8: Repeat rnd 2, using yarn E.

Fasten yarn.

Belts—Tailored and Tied

The right belt is not always easy to find. The color may be wrong, the price too high. When this happens, make a crocheted one.

A belt can be made in various ways to produce different designs. It can be tied or buckled. The texture may be smooth and silken or ridged and dull. By creating your own, you can have one with an individual touch.

Before you begin to crochet, decide how long the piece should be. Measure your waistline and to this figure add the right amount for the overlap or tie and for sewing a buckle in place.

This crocheted braid can be used to trim a suit as well as make a belt. Its interesting textural quality creates a sporty feeling. It resembles some of the corded belts that look so smart on a tailored dress.

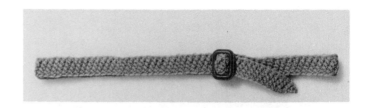

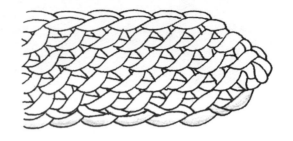

Information to Note

Size: Width 1 inch; length as desired

Materials: 1 ball 3-ply sportsweight yarn or a cotton cord (choose one with some firmness so there will be a distinctiveness to the stitches)
1 slip-through buckle

Tools: Afghan hook—Size 6
Tapestry needle

Gauge: 6 sts = 1 inch

Directions to Follow

Begin with 6 ch sts.

Row 1: Rep the following procedure across row: *Insert hook in the 1st st. Place yo hook. Draw through a lp.* Remember to keep all lps on hook.

Row 2: Do not turn work. Rep the following procedure: *Place yo hook. Draw through 2 lps. Insert hook under each horizontal strand across row.* For last lp, insert hook horizontally under last vertical strand.

Repeat rows 1 and 2 until the braid measures the required length.

Finishing belt: Turn under the lap end to form a point. Overhand edges together and hem the folded point in place. Use matching yarn. Sew the buckle to the other end with overhand stitches.

For a different look, try this soft, casual belt. It drapes nicely around the waist, adding a pretty touch to a dress or skirt.

Information to Note

Size: Length—waistline measurement plus 6 inches
Width—1¾ inches
Material: 1 skein Coats & Clark Lustersheen
Tool: Crochet hook—Size D
Gauge: 5 sts = 1 inch

Directions to Follow

Make a ch long enough to circle your waist loosely and add about 6 inches for the tie. Of course, if you would like a longer belt just make the ch longer.

Rnd 1: Crochet sc to within 1 ch of the end. Work 3 sc into last ch. Continue to crochet, working along other side. Take 3 sc in last st, sl st to 1st st.

Rnd 2: Repeat row 1, putting 2 sc into each of the 3 end stitches.

Rnd 3: Repeat rnd 2.

Rnd 4: Sc, sl st to 1st st.

Rnd 5: Turn. Work *1 dc, 1 sl st into each st around curve only, sc across long side. Repeat from *. Do this once. Fasten yarn. Work in ends of yarn and press lightly. Be sure to crochet evenly so belt will have a smooth, shiny surface.

Convenient Tote

Coats & Clark, Inc.

Shopping bags are usually more practical than pretty. When you find one that is both, you are fortunate. This one has a lacy look with a tasseled drawstring.

Information to Note

Size: 14 inches high

Materials: 8 ounces No. 629, Medium Pink, 3-ply Coats & Clark Red Heart® Heavy Rug Yarn

Tool: Crochet hook—Size G

Gauge: 7 dc = 2 inches
4 dc rows = 2¼ inches

Directions to Follow

Starting at bottom, ch 31, having 7 ch sts to 2 inches.

Rnd 1: Make 5 dc in 4th ch from hook, dc in each of next 26 ch; 6 dc in last ch; working along opposite side of starting chain, dc in each of next 26 ch. Join with sl st to top of ch-3—64 dc counting ch-3 as 1 dc.

Rnd 2: Ch 3, dc in joining, (2 dc in next dc) 5 times; dc in next 26 dc, (2 dc in next dc) 6 times; dc in next 26 dc. Join as before—76 sts.

Rnd 3: Ch 3, dc in next dc, (2 dc in next dc) 8 times; dc in next 30 dc, (2 dc in next dc) 8 times; dc in next 28 dc. Join—92 sts.

Rnd 4: Ch 3, dc in back lp of next dc and in back lp of each dc around. Join.

Rnds 5–9: Ch 3, dc through both lps of next dc and through both lps of each dc around. Join.

Rnd 10: Ch 1, sc in joining; *draw lp on hook up to measure ½ inch, yo and draw through lp on hook, insert hook between the ½-inch lp and the single strand behind it and draw a lp through (there are now 2 lps on hook), yo and draw through the 2 lps on hook, make another knot st, skip next 3 dc, sc in next dc—knot st lp completed. Rep from * around to last 3 dc, make 2 knot sts. Join with sl st to 1st sc—23 knot st lps. An illustration of the knot st is shown on page 92.

Rnds 11–24: Draw lp on hook up to reach knot at center of 1st knot st lp, sl st in knot at center of same lp, ch 1, sc in same place; make 2 knot sts, *sc in knot at center of next knot st lp, make 2 knot sts. Rep from * around. Join to first sc—23 knot st lps.

Rnd 25: Work as for previous rnd until the first sc is completed, ch 3, *sc in knot at center of next knot st lp, ch 3. Rep from * around. Join.

Rnd 26: Ch 3, dc in each of next 3 ch, *working in back lp only, dc in next sc, dc in next 3 ch. Rep from * around. Join to top of ch-3.

Rnds 27–28: Ch 3, dc in next dc and in each dc around. Join. Fasten off.

Cord: Cut 2 strands, each 10 yards long. Fold in half and knot loose strands together. Place folded end over doorknob or hook. Place a pencil through knotted end and twist yarn in one direction. Remove pencil and, holding yarn taut at all times, fold in half. Release folded end a little at a time and it will twist into a cord. Tie a strand of yarn around cut end of twisted cord 4½ inches up from the end. Cut 6 strands of yarn 10 inches long and draw halfway through cord above tie strand to make a heavier tassel. Wind a double strand of yarn ½ inch down from top of tassel to secure. Thread opposite end of cord in and out between dc's of Rnd 27 sts as desired for drawstring. Now cut 10 strands, each 10 inches long, and draw halfway through lp of folded end of cord and complete tassel as before. Trim tassels.

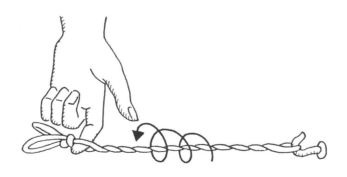

Handy Shawl

Coats & Clark, Inc.

There always seems to be a place in one's wardrobe for a shawl. Giving it a distinctive touch is important. This one has a knotted texture and a two-tone effect.

Information to Note

Size: Shawl is 72 inches across long edge of triangle, 38 inches at center back, including border

Materials: 9 ounces No. 722, light pink, Coats & Clark Red Heart® Art. E. 281 7 ounces No. 737, Bright Pink, 3-ply Coats & Clark Red Heart® Sofspun Baby Yarn Art. E. 274

Tool: Crochet hook—Size H

Gauge: 1 knot st lp = 1 inch 2 rows = 1 inch

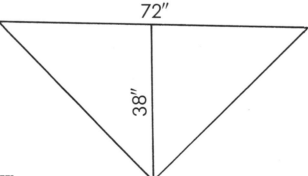

72"

38"

Directions to Follow

With 1 strand of each color held together and starting at lower point, ch 6.

Row 1: Draw lp on hook up to measure ⅝ inch, yo and draw through lp on hook, insert hook between the ⅝-inch lp and the single strand behind it, and draw a lp through (2 lps on hook), yo and draw through all lps on hook. You have made a knot st; make another knot st, then sl st in last ch of ch-6—1 knot st lp. Ch 4, turn.

Row 2: Make 2 knot sts, sc in center of knot st lp, make 2 knot sts, tr in next ch of ch-6—2 knot st lps. Ch 4, turn.

Row 3: (2 knot sts, sc in center of next knot st lp) twice; 2 knot sts, tr in top of ch-4—3 knot st lps. Ch 4, turn.

Row 4: *2 knot sts, sc in center of next knot st lp. Rep from *, end with 2 knot sts, tr in top of ch-4—1 knot st lp more than on previous row. Ch 4, turn.

Rep Row 4 until 72 knot st lps are on row. Ch 6, turn.

Next Row: Sc in center of first knot st lp, *ch 3, sc in center of next knot st lp. Rep from * to last knot st, ch 2, tr in top of ch-4. Ch 2, turn.

Border: Rnd 1: Hdc in same place, ch 1, *draw up a lp around stem of last st, yo, skip next ch or st, draw up a loop in next ch or st, yo and draw through all 4 lps on hook, ch 1. Rep from * to next corner, working along next 2 side edges, **knot sts, skip 5/8 inch along edge, sc in edge. Rep from ** to the ch-2 at beg of rnd. Join with sl st to top of ch-2. Make 3 knot sts, turn.

Next Row: Working along side edges only, sc in center of next knot st lp, *2 knot sts, sc in center of next knot st lp. Rep from * across, end with 3 knot sts, sl st in corner. Fasten off.

Last row: Turn and attach the 2 strands in 3rd knot st, ch 1, sc in same place, *(2 knot sts, sc in same place as last sc) twice; 1 knot st, sc in center of next knot st lp. Rep from * across, making last group in 2nd knot st of last 3 knot sts. Fasten off.

Colorful Jacket

Coats & Clark, Inc.

Granny squares give this classic jacket a different look. Of course, if you wish, the squares can be made in subdued colors.

Information to Note

Sizing: Directions are given for Small [8–10] size; changes for Medium [12–14] and Large [16] sizes are in brackets

Materials: 8 ounces No. 283, Pantile Brown
6 ounces No. 111, Eggshell
4 ounces No. 36
4 ounces No. 12, Black
All yarns 2-ply Coats & Clark Red Heart® sports yarn Art. E. 281

Tools: Crochet hook:
Size E for Small
Size F for Medium
Size G for Large
Tapestry needle

Gauge: Each motif is 4 [4 1/4, 4 1/2]-inch square

Directions to Follow

Right Back Section Motif A (Make 6): With E [F, G] hook and Eggshell, ch 5. Join with sl st to form ring.

Rnd 1 (right side): Ch 3 to count as 1 dc, 3 dc in ring, ch 1 for corner sp, (4 dc in ring, ch 1 for corner sp) 3 times. Join to top of ch-3. Break off and fasten.

Rnd 2: Attach Pantile Brown to any corner sp, ch 3 in same sp make dc, ch 2 and 2 dc—starting corner group made; *dc between next 2 dc, **dc between last dc and next dc. Repeat from ** to next corner sp; in corner sp make 2 dc, ch 2, and 2 dc. Repeat from * twice; dc between next 2 dc, *** dc between last and next dc. Repeat from *** to next corner. Join to top of ch-3. Break off and fasten.

Rnd 3: Attach Wood Brown to any corner sp and repeat Rnd 2.

Rnd 4: With Pantile Brown, repeat Rnd 2.

Rnd 5: With Eggshell, repeat Rnd 2.

Motif B (Make 6): Work same as Motif A, using colors in the following order: *Rnd 1:* Black. *Rnd 2:* Wood Brown. *Rnd 3:* Pantile Brown. *Rnd 4:* Eggshell. *Rnd 5:* Black.

Sewing through back lps only throughout, sew the 12 motifs together, following Diagram 1 for placement.

Edging: Starting to work across long edge of section with right side facing, attach Pantile Brown to corner sp.

Rnd 1: Ch 1, make 3 sc in corner sp, *sc in each dc to corner sp of same motif, sc in sp of same motif, sc in corner sp of next motif. Repeat from * to next corner sp of section, make 3 sc in corner sp, continue to work across remaining 3 edges in same way. Join to first sc. Break off and fasten.

NOTE: Hereafter, pin each finished section to measurements, dampen, and leave to dry.

Left Back Section. Work as for Right Back Section, following Diagram 2 for placement of motifs.

Sew center back seam.

Left Front: Work same as Right Back Section.

Right Front: Work as for Left Back Section.

Leaving first motif free at lower edge for side slit and 2 motifs free at top

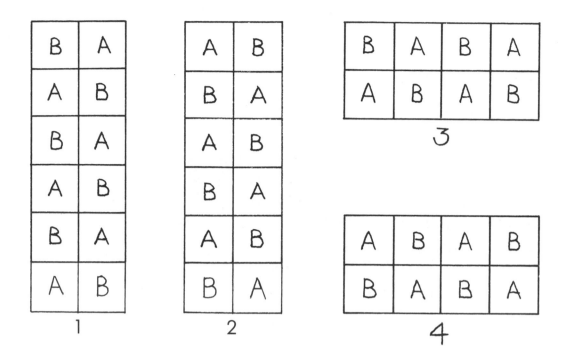

B	A
A	B
B	A
A	B
B	A
A	B

1

A	B
B	A
A	B
B	A
A	B
B	A

2

B	A	B	A
A	B	A	B

3

A	B	A	B
B	A	B	A

4

for armhole, sew remaining 3 motifs together for side seams. Starting at armhole edge, sew 5½ [5¾, 6]-inch shoulder seams. For Large size only: Work 1 row of sc along each front edge.

Right Sleeve Back Section: Make 4 motifs of A and 4 Motifs of B. Sew the 8 motifs together, following Diagram 3 for placement of motifs. Work edging same as edging of Right Back Section.

Front Section: Work as for Right Sleeve Back Section, following Diagram 4 for placement of motifs. Work edging as before.

Sew underarm sleeve seam. Leaving first motif free at lower edge for slit, sew top sleeve seam. Sew in sleeve.

Left Sleeve Back Section: Work as for Right Sleeve Front Section.

Front Section: Work as for Right Sleeve Back Section.

Sew sleeve seams as before. Sew in sleeve.

Outer Edging: With wrong side facing, attach Pantile Brown at center back of neck.

Rnd 1: Ch 1, sc in same place, sc in each sc around entire outer edge, making 3 sc in each corner. Join to first sc. Break off and fasten.

Sleeve Edging: Attach Pantile Brown at underarm seam and work Edging same as Outer Edging.

NOTE: Pin each finished section to measurements, dampen, and leave to dry.

BLOCKING MEASUREMENTS

SIZES	Small 8–10	Medium [12–14]	Large [16]
Body Bust Size (in Inches)	31½–32½	34–36	38
Actual Crocheting Measurements (in Inches)			
Bust	35	37	40
Width across back	17	18½	19½
Width across each front, including edging	8½	9¼	10¼
Length from shoulder to lower edge	24½	26	27½
Width across each sleeve	17	18½	19½
Length of sleeve seam	16¼	17¼	18½

One finished back or front section, 8½ × 24½, [9 × 26], [9¾ × 27½].

One finished sleeve section, 8½ × 16 ½, [9 × 17½], [9¾ × 18¾].

Tie (Make 2): Cut 3 strands of Pantile Brown, each 6 yards long. Fold in half and knot ends together. Place folded end over a hook or doorknob. Place a pencil through other end and twist yarn. When yarn is tightly twisted, remove pencil and, holding yarn taut all the time, fold it in half. Release folded end a little at a time and it will automatically spring into a twisted cord. Tie open ends into a knot and trim. Sew to front edge of jacket between the 2nd and 3rd motifs from top edge.

A Cozy Hat

Coats & Clark, Inc.

This casual hat has several interesting features. It is made with a rolled brim, which gives it a certain trimness. And although crocheted, it looks knitted.

Information to Note

Material: 5 ounces No. 123, Rust, 4-ply Coats & Clark Red Heart® "Sparkling" hand knitting yarn, Art. E. 267-S

Tools: Crochet hook—Size I
Tapestry needle

Gauge: Single strand: 3 sc = 1 inch
Double strand: 5 hdc = 2 inches

Directions to Follow

Crown: Starting at center top with single strand, ch 2.

Rnd 1: Make 6 sc in 2nd ch from hook. Do not join rnds, but to indicate beg of each rnd bring a thread in contrasting color up between last and first st.

Rnd 2: 2 sc in each sc around—12 sc.

Rnd 3: *2 sc in next sc—1 sc increased; sc in next sc. Rep from * around —6 sc increased.

Rnd 4: Increasing 6 sc evenly spaced, sc in each sc around. Rep 4th rnd until there are 48 sc on rnd.

Rnds 5–7: Increasing 4 sc evenly spaced, sc in each sc around. There are 60 sc on last rnd.

Rnd 8: Sc in each sc around.

Rep last rnd until length from center top is 5¾ inches.

Next rnd: *Sc in next 10 sc, draw up a lp in each of next 2 sc, yo and draw through all 3 lps on hook—1 sc decreased. Rep from * around. Join with sl st to 1st sc—55 sc. Break off and fasten.

Brim: With 2 strands of yarn held tog, ch 21 to measure 8½ inches.

Row 1: Hdc in 3rd ch from hook and in each ch across—19 hdc. Do not count the ch-2 as 1 hdc. Ch 2, turn.

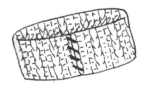

Row 2: Hdc in back lp of each hdc across. Ch 2, turn.

Rep 2nd row until piece measures 23 inches. Break off and fasten.

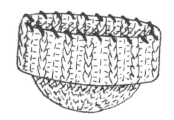

Sew narrow edges together to form a ring. Sew long edges together. Sew long brim seam to last rnd of crown, holding in to fit. Measure 1½ inches up from last rnd of crown, and fold brim up to this point.

Mile-a-Minute Lap Robe

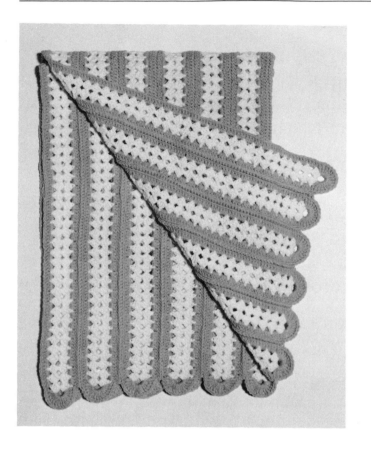

Just as its name implies, this coverlet is quick to make and easy to handle. Made of lacy strips, it offers possibilities for creativity. The panels can be made of any length and in different color combinations. For this lap robe two colors have been used, blue bordering a center of white. For variation you might crochet for a solid color effect or alternate a solid one with two-tone panel. Another interesting feature is the scalloped ends.

Information to Note

Size: Lap robe shown here 36 × 58 inches with 12 panels
For an afghan, the size is 54 × 76 inches with 17 panels

Materials: 6 skeins 4-ply blue Aunt Mary's yarn
5 skeins 4-ply white Aunt Mary's yarn

Tool: Crochet hook—Size H

Directions to Follow

Panel: To crochet center portion of panels, begin this way:
   Row 1: Ch 7. Sl st in 1st ch to form ring. Ch 3. Turn.
   Row 2: Made 2 dc, ch 3, 3 dc, ch 3, turn.
   Row 3: Work 3 dc in space, ch 3, 3 dc in same space, 1 dc in last st of ch of previous row, ch 3, turn.

Row 4: Continue to crochet, repeating row 3 until the desired length is reached. It will be easier to handle a panel if you keep it rolled. This will also keep your work from stretching.

Border for Panel: Start in any sp on side of panel, using the blue yarn. Make 3 dc between each shell. Continue around strip. At each end, crochet 15 tr sts.

Joining: Put 2 strips together with wrong sides together. Use a sc, matching stitch for stitch. Crocheting with the wrong sides together produces a ridged effect between the panels.

Up-Front Bag

This type of bag has been popular with sportspeople for some time. It frees the hands when shopping and snacking and at the same time provides a certain amount of security for personal possessions. Although the bags for sportswear are usually made of black nylon, you can have one in your favorite color if you crochet it.

Information to Note

Size: Bag approximately 6 × 6 inches
Belt—waist measure plus lap of about 4 inches; width 1½ inches

Materials: 2 balls firm cotton yarn
1 flat button
1 buckle

Tools: Afghan hook—No. 6
Tapestry needle

Gauge: 5 sc = 1 inch

Directions to Follow

Belt: Begin by crocheting the belt and then adding the bag. Use a basic afghan stitch. Ch 6 stitches.

Row 1: Insert the hook in the 2nd ch from the hook. With yo hook, draw a lp through the ch st. Continue the procedure to end of row. The lps are left on the hook.

Row 2: Remove lps from the hook without turning the work. Do this by placing yo hook and draw a lp through the 1st st. Repeat the following procedure until only 1 ch remains on hook: *Place yo hook, and draw it through 2 lps.*

Row 3: Working from right to left, insert hook under the vertical stitch. Put yo hook. Draw through the lp. Continue this way to end of row. There should be 6 sts on hook.

Row 4: Rep row 2.

Continue to crochet until desired length is reached, repeating rows 3 and 4. To finish the belt with a pointed end, decrease sts at each side until 1 lp remains. Fasten yarn.

Bag: Decide how you are going to wear the bag. Mark the position on the belt. Then, working with the wrong side of the belt facing you and from right to left, pick up 28 lps. Attach yarn. Crochet in afghan sts for 11 inches.

Row 1: Remove the lps from the hook. Place yo hook and draw through the 1st lp. Then repeat the following procedure until only 1 ch remains on hook: *Place yo hook and draw it through 2 lps.* Make 1 ch.

Row 2: Working from right to left, insert hook under the vertical st. Put yo hook. Draw through the lp. Continue across row this way.

For the remainder of the work, rep rows 1 and 2 until piece measures 11 inches. Fasten yarn.

Flap: Work on wrong side of belt. Pick up 28 loops, working from right to left. Attach yarn. Crochet in afghan sts until flap measures 2½ inches.

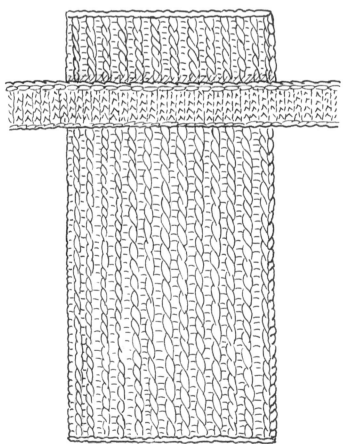

Use the same procedure that you used for rows 1 and 2 in making the bag. For last row, remove lps from hook until 1 lp remains. Fasten yarn.

Finishing: Fold bag portion up so end meets lower edge of belt. Wrong sides are together. Join sides with sc.

Place a row of sc around flap and belt to add a bit of firmness.

Add a ch loop to the flap and

53

a button to the bag. Sew a buckle to one end of the belt.

To hold the end of the belt in place, add a narrow loop. On the top edge, 5 sts from buckle, make a sl st. Then crochet 8 chs, the width of belt. Fasten to the lower edge of the belt with a sl st 5 sts from buckle. Finish loop with sc in each ch. Fasten yarn and weave end into belt.

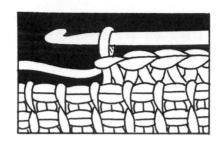

PART II

Knitting

Guidelines

Knitting seems to have a universal appeal. The clicking of knitting needles fascinates many as they watch a ball of yarn become an attractive article. On the following pages you will find some suggestions to help you create just that transformation.

Getting Started

Before you begin the knitting process, the yarn should be *wound into a ball.* In the Crocheting section of this book, page 2, a description of this procedure is given.

Casting On Stitches. Before the knitting actually begins, stitches must be put on one of the needles you are using. There are several ways to do this. The one suggested here can be used not only to start the knitting, but also when it is necessary to cast on stitches in the middle of a piece. This method is referred to as *knitting on stitches.* It also allows you to handle the needles as you will for the actual knitting.

Holding the Needles seems to be a personal matter. Each person seems to have her own way. In case you haven't decided how you like to knit

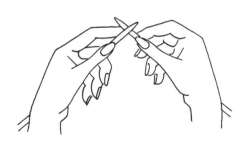

or you want to make a change, then try this position. Work with the hands above the needles. It is the easiest way and does not require as much manipulation of the fingers. The needle in the left hand is placed between the thumb and first finger.

Holding the yarn is a right-hand duty. The yarn runs through the fingers. Put it over the first finger, under the middle and ring fingers, and around the little finger. The first finger moves the yarn around the needle. The middle and ring fingers regulate the flow of yarn. You do not want to knit the stitches too tight or too loose, and at the same time you do not want to stretch the yarn or have the stitches fall off the needle.

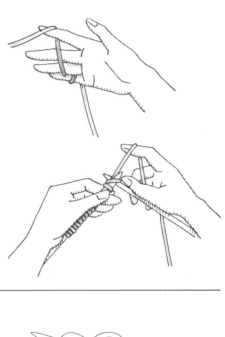

To start casting on, make a *slip knot or loop* at the end of the yarn. To do this, hold the yarn a short distance from the end, between the thumb and first finger. Make a small circle of yarn by pulling the ball end of the yarn over the short end. Draw the ball end of the yarn through the circle with the knitting needle. Pull ends of yarn in opposite directions to draw the loop smaller. It should fit the needle closely.

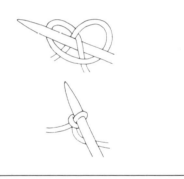

To take the first stitch, put the needle in your left hand. Then pick up the other needle with the right hand and insert it in the loop under the left-hand needle. Place the yarn under and over the right-hand needle (A). Pull yarn through loop, keeping the loop on the left-hand needle (B). To put the stitch you have just made on the left-hand needle twist it and slip it over needle, keeping the right-hand needle on top of the left-hand one (C). When the stitch is in place, remove the right-hand needle from its on-top placement. Slip it under the left-hand needle and

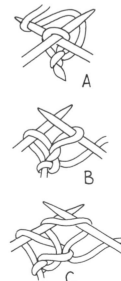

through the stitch. You can now knit the next stitch. Continue to work this way until the necessary number of stitches have been cast on.

The Basic Stitches

Although it may seem improbable, there are only two basic stitches—*knit* and *purl*. They can be used and combined in such a variety of ways that the results are almost unbelievable. Perhaps you will want to try your creative ability.

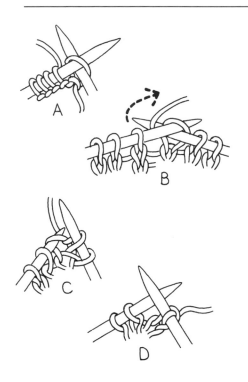

Knit Stitch. Knitting begins with this stitch. With the needle bearing the cast-on stitches in the left hand, pick up the other needle and yarn with the right hand. Insert point of needle into the front of the first stitch and behind the left-hand needle (A).

Wind the yarn under and over the right-hand needle (B). Draw the yarn through the stitch (C), knitting a new stitch on the right-hand needle. Carefully slip the stitch off the left-hand needle (D). Continue to work in this way, making a row of knit stitches.

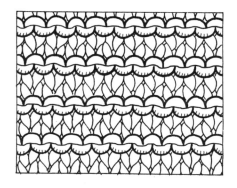

A *Garter Stitch* pattern results from knitting 2 rows of knit stitches. It is often called plain knitting. When you have knitted off all of the stitches on the left-hand needle, exchange needles. Transfer the empty one to your right hand.

To begin the second row, turn the work. Slip or knit the first stitch. Then continue to knit the remaining stitches as you did the first row. The 2 rows make a raised ridge and appear the same on both sides.

Purl Stitch. Although this stitch plays a very important part in knitting, it is never used alone. It is always combined in some way with a knit stitch.

To purl, hold the needles in the same way as for the knit stitch with these exceptions: the yarn is held in front of the work instead of in back, and the right-hand needle is placed in front of the left-hand needle. Insert the needle in the stitch from the back (A). Place yarn around the needle following the diagram shown here (B). Slip old stitch off the left-hand needle (C). Continue to purl all stitches this way.

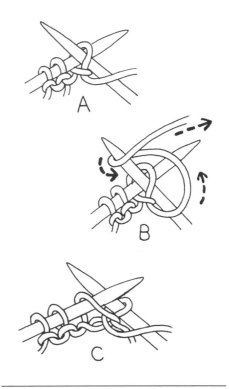

Stockinette Stitch. When a row of knit stitches is combined with a row of purl stitches, a special effect results. The rows are alternated, first a row of knit stitches and then a row of purl.

Begin with a row of knit stitches. At the end of the row, turn the work and bring the yarn to the front of the work in order to begin purling.

When the row of purling is completed, prepare for a row of knit stitches. Transfer the work and turn it. Put the yarn in back and knit the row. Follow this alternating routine for as many rows as required.

In case you forget which row you are working on, remember that when the smooth surface with vertical rows of chain stitches is toward you, the row is knitted. Purl the row when the surface is rough and appears as closely placed horizontal rows of garter stitches. The Stocki-

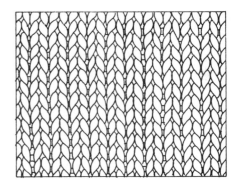

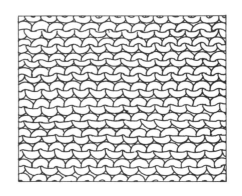

nette Stitch creates no right or wrong side, although each side looks completely different.

Ribbing. This stitch pattern offers another way to combine knit and purl stitches. To create the effect, alternate knit and purl stitches as you knit the row. For instance, alternating 2 knit stitches and 2 purl stitches creates the look shown here.

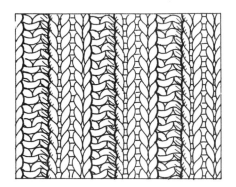

Start by knitting the required number of stitches in the regular manner. Then bring the yarn to the front of the needle and purl the necessary number of stitches. Return the yarn to the back and knit the next sequence of stitches. Continue knitting and purling until the row is completed. In making the next row, remember that the knitted stitches will be purled and the purl stitches knitted.

The End

The knitting must always come to an end. At that time a technique called *binding or casting off* is used. Usually this is done on the wrong side. The stitches should be worked loosely enough so that the bound-off edge will have the necessary amount of stretch.

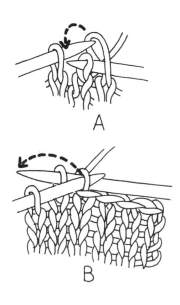

To bind off on the knit side, slip or knit loosely the first stitch. Knit the second stitch loosely. Two stitches are now on the right-hand needle. To remove the first stitch, pass the left-hand needle through the left side of the first stitch on the right-hand needle (A). Lift the first stitch and pass it over the second stitch and the tip of the right-hand needle (B), dropping it from the needle, leaving 1 stitch on the needle.

Knit the next stitch loosely. Again there are 2 stitches on the right-hand needle. Slip the first stitch over the second stitch and tip of needle. One stitch remains on the needle. Continue this procedure until only 1 stitch is left on needle. Cut the yarn about 3 inches from the stitch. Slip the end through the stitch on the needle (C). Remove the needle.

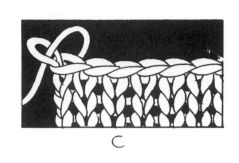

C

To bind off on the purl side, use the same basic technique except that the position of the yarn must be changed. Purl 2 stitches. Move the yarn to the back of this work. Continue as for the knit side. Slip the left-hand needle through the left side of the first stitch on the right-hand needle. Pass the first stitch over the second and the tip of the needle. Work this way, remembering to carry the yarn to the back after each new purl stitch.

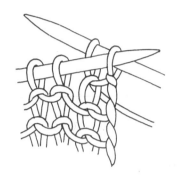

To bind off ribbing, use the knit and purl process, alternating in the proper sequence. This allows the ribbing to maintain the close ribbed effect.

Special Techniques

Knitting on Circular Needles. Although most knitting is done on straight needles, there are times when knitting on circular needles is necessary to create a certain look or to make a certain detail easier to do.

After casting on the required number of stitches, lay the needle on a flat surface. Check the placement of the stitches. Be certain that there are no twisted stitches. Always keep the finished edge of the stitches inside and the looped edge on the outside.

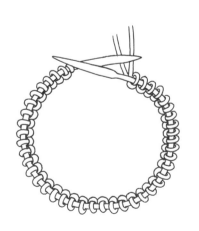

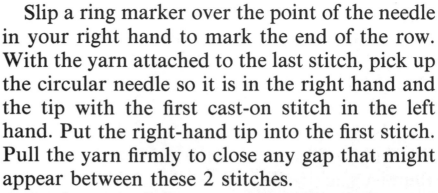

Slip a ring marker over the point of the needle in your right hand to mark the end of the row. With the yarn attached to the last stitch, pick up the circular needle so it is in the right hand and the tip with the first cast-on stitch in the left hand. Put the right-hand tip into the first stitch. Pull the yarn firmly to close any gap that might appear between these 2 stitches.

At the end of the row, move the marker and continue to knit round and round.

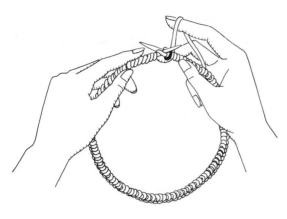

Flat Knitting on a Circular Needle. A large flat piece of knitting is sometimes difficult to handle on straight needles. Working on a circular needle seems to make it easier. Instead of working in the round, the knitting is done back and forth as you would on straight needles. There are, however, a few changes in the procedure.

Hold the tip of the needle with the last cast-on stitch in your left hand and the other end with the first cast-on stitch in your right hand. Place the right-hand tip into the last stitch. Start to knit in the usual way. Continue to the starting point. Instead of working round and round, stop at the end of the row and turn the needle so the wrong side of the work is toward you. Continue to work back and forth.

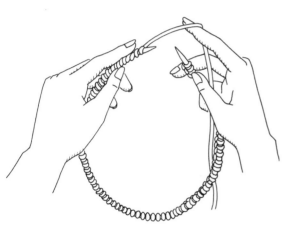

Understanding the Directions

Knowing the mechanics of knitting is not enough. You must also be able to interpret the directions that allow you to knit an interesting article. In order to help you, some of the abbreviations and terms that are used are explained here.

Abbreviations. Before you begin to knit an article, be sure to read the directions carefully. If there is an abbreviation, check its meaning.

beg	beginning	P	purl
dec	decrease	Pb	purl into back of stitch
dec L	decrease left		
dec R	decrease right	rep	repeat
in(s)	inch(es)	* or **	repeat directions in same order following * or **
incl	inclusive		
inc	increase		
inc L	increase left	* * or ( )	repeat directions found between asterisks or parentheses
inc R	increase right		
K	knit		
Kb	knit into back of stitch		
		RH	right-hand needle
LH	left-hand	rnd	round
M1	make 1 stitch	sc	single crochet
pnso or p.n.s.o.	pass or pull next stitch over	sl, s	slip
		st(s)	stitch(es)
psso or p.s.s.o.	pass or pull slipped stitch over	st st	stockinette stitch
		tog	together
		yo or o	yarn over
pu 1	pick up 1 stitch		

Special Terms. Understanding knitting terminology is important. It always makes following directions easier.

Attaching yarn is usually something that must be done when knitting an article. Introducing the new end should be done as inconspicuously as possible and at the same time provide strong joining. Whenever possible, attach the yarn with a knot at the beginning of a row (A). The ends can be concealed by weaving the threads up and down along the edge (B).

If it is necessary to *join yarn of a different color mid-row* with a knot, the knot can be untied on the wrong side when the article is completed and the ends woven into the knitting. Slip the right-hand end into several stitches to the left, the left-hand end in the stitches to the right (C). The ends will be invisible when carefully interwoven.

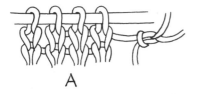

A

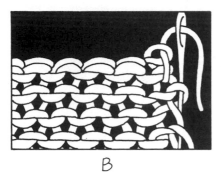

B

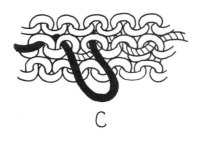

C

Changing colors must be done carefully so no holes appear at the changeover. To prevent this, twist one color around the other at the joining. Carry the yarn you are not using loosely across the work on the wrong side. Pick up the new color from under the one that is to be dropped.

Placing a Marker. Just as you mark your place when reading, you should also do it when knitting when working on such a procedure as increasing or marking the end of a row. The marker can be a piece of yarn in a

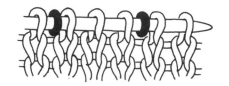

contrasting color or a plastic ring. Place it on the right-hand needle at the specified spot. Slip the ring from one needle to the other as the knitting progresses. If you are using yarn, make a slip knot to hold the yarn in place. Leave ends of about 2 inches.

Shaping a Piece. This can be done by reducing or adding stitches. To *decrease* the number of stitches, two methods can be used.

For the first, *2 stitches are knitted together.* Put the right-hand needle through the front of the second stitch and then through the first on the left-hand needle (A). Make a regular knit stitch, drawing the yarn through both stitches. Slip the 2 stitches off needle as 1. The 2 stitches can be seen grouped together under the needle (B).

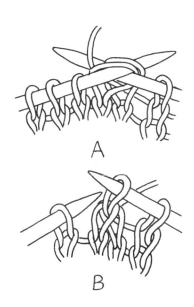

To *decrease in purling,* purl 2 stitches together.

The second method for decreasing is done by slipping a stitch. When you see the abbreviation "psso," you will know what to do. Move 1 stitch from the left-hand needle to the right-hand one without knitting (A). Then knit the next stitch. Bring the slipped stitch over the knitted one, using the left-hand needle (B), and finally over the right.

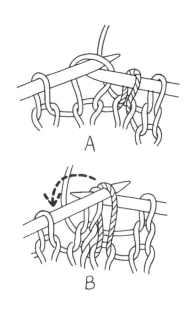

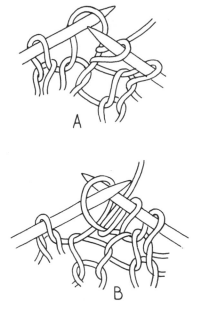

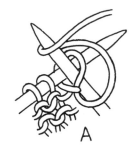

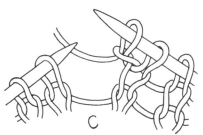

To increase in knitting, knit first into the front of the stitch in the usual way, but do not remove the old stitch from the left-hand needle (A). Instead, maneuver the right-hand needle under the left-hand one. Knit into the back of the same stitch to create the extra stitch (B). Then slip the old stitch off the left-hand needle, leaving 2 stitches on the right-hand needle instead of 1 (C).

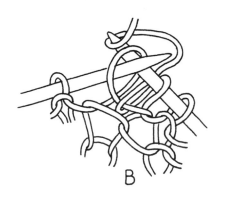

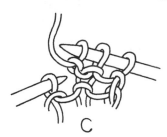

To increase in purling, purl into the front of the stitch in the regular way, leaving the stitch on the needle (A). Work the extra stitch by *purling into the back* of the same stitch (B). Slip the old stitch off the left-hand needle, leaving 2 stitches on the right-hand needle instead of 1 (C).

Blocking puts the final touch to a knitted piece. Not only does it help in the shaping, but it also gives a professional look to an amateurish bit of knitting. In the crocheting section, page 16, you will find some tips for successful blocking.

Slip a Stitch. These few words indicate that a stitch is to be moved from the left-hand needle to the right-hand needle without knitting. Sometimes it is done at the beginning of a row; at others, mid-row. Usually a stitch is slipped purlwise from the left-hand needle to the right-hand needle into the front of the stitch. Then transfer the stitch without knitting or purling it. Keep the yarn in back of the work.

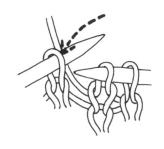

Yarn in Front. When knitting certain stitch patterns it is necessary to bring the yarn from the back of the work to the front. Slip the yarn between the two needles.

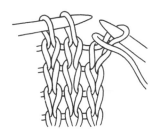

Yarn Over. Knitting depends on putting the yarn over the needle. Before a knit stitch, bring yarn forward by placing it under and over the right-hand needle (A). Then knit the stitch. When the following row is knitted, the stitch will appear as in B.

For a *yarn over when purling,* wrap yarn completely around the right-hand needle. Then purl the stitch (C).

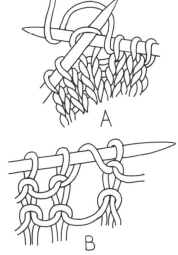

Picking Up Stitches. Sometimes one section of the item you are making is knitted into another, such as a sleeve to the body of the sweater. Work from right to left with the right side of knitting toward you. Hold the knitting in your left hand with the needle and yarn in the right hand.

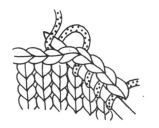

Insert the needle in the first stitch in the row just below the edge. Place the yarn around the needle as if you were knitting a stitch. Pull the yarn through, forming a loop or stitch on right-hand needle. Continue this procedure until the required number of stitches have been picked up.

Correcting Mistakes

One doesn't like to think about mistakes, but they do happen. In case a stitch is dropped, twisted, or made incorrectly, here are a few suggestions for correcting the error without too much trouble.

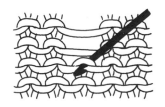

Dropped Stitches. When a stitch has fallen off the needle accidentally, work with a crochet hook for the best results. Put the hook in the dropped stitch. Draw the horizontal strand of yarn of the row above through the loop. Proceed in this way until you reach the row of stitches on the needle. Slip the picked-up stitch onto the needle. Be careful not to twist it.

When working with the *stockinette stitch,* keep the right or smooth side toward you. But if you are knitting *garter stitches,* turn the work from side to side so the stitch design will be maintained.

Twisted stitches should be avoided. They disturb the evenness of the knitting. When you are knitting correctly, the yarn always passes over the needle in the same direction with the stitches lined up evenly on the needle. In checking the position of the stitches, be sure that the part of the loop that is in front of the needle is closer to the point (A). If it looks as it does in B, then the stitch is twisted and must be turned.

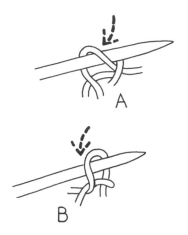

Ripping back is not a pleasant activity. However, there are times when it must be done. When the mistake happens in the row you are working on, it is necessary to take the knitting off the needle. Begin by returning the stitches to the left-hand needle. To do this, slip the needle into the loop or stitch through which the yarn is passing. Pull the right-hand needle out of the last stitch that was knitted, leaving 1 less stitch on this needle. Continue this way until the point of the mistake is reached.

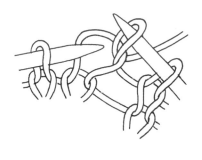

If you do not realize that there is a mistake until the work has been turned, the stitches should be ripped back in the same way, stitch by stitch, row by row. If this seems tedious, you can remove the work from the needles and ravel. If you decide to do this, then be careful when you pick up the stitches—they twist easily. To avoid this, ravel the last row stitch by stitch, putting each stitch on a smaller needle as it is raveled. Then knit the stitches onto the regular needle.

Tools and Yarns

The equipment needs of knitting are simple. A pair of needles and a bit of yarn are all you really need. There are, however, a few gadgets that you may find helpful.

Knitting needles are made in a variety of types, sizes, and materials. There are straight ones and circular ones. And the straight needles can be made with single or double points.

The sizes range from 0, the smallest, to 50, the largest in U.S.A. sizing, and in different lengths. At times the needles have been made from such material as bone, wood, and steel. Today aluminum and plastic seem to be favored.

Although directions usually suggest an appropriate size, there are a few other factors to consider. If the needles are too large for the yarn, the knitting will be loose, allowing the knitting to stretch, and if the needles are too small, the knitting seems too firm.

The length of the needle should be checked. Although the number of stitches influences your choice, the length of your arm and the type of chair used play their part. You want to be comfortable, and at the same time avoid any crowding of the stitches. It is difficult to watch the development of the design if this happens.

Some knitters find certain gadgets helpful but not necessary. *Protectors* for the points of the needles offer safety. Colored plastic rings can be used as *markers* to designate the place where a design detail changes. Special *holders* for stitches simplify certain procedures.

Counters and *gauges* of various types contribute to accuracy.

Of course, you should have something to hold your knitting supplies. A bag with several dividing sections will keep the different items neatly organized and in good condition. Directions for one you can make are found on page 117.

Yarns. In the Crocheting section on page 18, you will find some information about selecting the proper yarn. Developing a discriminating touch is a great asset. The beauty of the knitting is not only in the color of the yarn but also in the appropriateness of the texture.

Items to Knit

On the following pages you will find a collection of articles that you can knit as gifts or for yourself, ranging from a turtleneck for your dog to slipper socks for yourself. Each one has been chosen for ease of construction and the possibilities for creative expression.

Baby Pullover

The bulky effect gives this sweater a very grown-up look. Made in one piece, it features a garter-stitch trim and a tab closing. Although easy to make, it does require attention to design details.

Brunswick Yarns

Information to Note

Size: 6 months (1, 2, 3 years)
  Finished chest measurements 20 (21, 22, 23) inches
Material: 1 (2, 2, 2) pull skeins, 100 grams, Brunswick Windrush®, 1 button
Tools: Knitting needles—No. 8 Crochet hook—No. 6 (G), aluminum Tapestry needle
Gauge: 5 sts = 1 inch over stockinette st

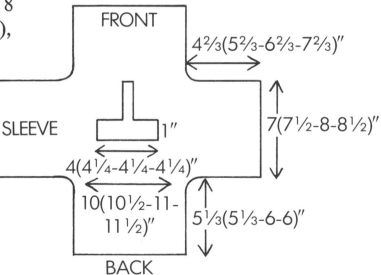

Directions to Follow

Pullover: Knit in 1 piece. Cast on 50 (53, 55, 58) sts.
  Rows 1–8: Work in garter st, knitting every row.
  Following Rows: Change to stockinette st and work even until piece measures 5 (5½, 6, 6½) ins.

Next Rows: Inc 1 st at each end of every other row 3 times—56 (59, 61, 64) sts.

Next 2 Rows: At beg, cast on 20 (25, 30, 35) sts.

Then, working first and last 4 sts in garter st with the sts between in stockinette st, work even on 96 (109, 121, 134) sts for 2 (2¼, 2½, 2¾) ins.

Next Row: Work across first 34 (46, 46, 52) sts, keeping pattern, place marker, K 28 (29, 29, 30) sts, place marker, work across last 34 (40, 46, 52) sts in pattern.

Continue pattern for 8 rows, working garter st on all sts between markers and on 4 edge sts.

Shape Neck: Work across to marker, K 4, bind off next 20 (21, 21, 22) sts, K 4, slip marker, work to end.

Continue working only on left side of neck. Work for 1 in, keeping pattern ending at neck edge.

Next Row: Cast on 10 (10, 10, 11) sts, K 14 (14, 14, 15) sts before marker, work to last 4 sts, K 4.

Continue for 8 rows, keeping garter st at cuff and neck edges.

Then continue for 2 more ins, keeping only the first and last 4 sts in garter st and all other sts in stockinette st, ending at sleeve edge.

***Next Row:* Bind off first 20 (25, 30, 35) sts. Work across next 28 (29, 30, 32) sts and place on holder. Cut yarn.

Right Side: Attach yarn at neck edge and work to match left side to **, reversing shaping and ending at sleeve edge.

Next Row: Bind off first 20 (25, 30, 35) sts, work across to end in stockinette st, inc 0 (1, 1, 0) st at end of row, then work across sts from left front holder. Dec 1 st each side of every other row 3 times—50 (53, 55, 58) sts.

Continue in stockinette st until front measures same as back from underarm to garter st border.

Next 8 rows: Work in garter st. Bind off.

Finishing: Sew back and front tog along sleeve and side seams.

Loop and Button: Attach yarn at left front neck. Chain 6 sts for button loop. Fasten end securely to sweater. Sew button to right neck edge.

Companion Cardigan

Brunswick Yarns

By opening up the front, the baby pullover has been converted into a cardigan. Adding bows gives it a pretty touch.

Information to Note

Size: 6 months (1, 2, 3 years)

Material: 1 (2, 2, 2) pull skeins, 100 grams, Brunswick Windrush®

Tools: Knitting needles—No. 8
Crochet hook—No. 6 (G), aluminum
Tapestry needle

Gauge: 5 sts = 1 inch over stockinette st

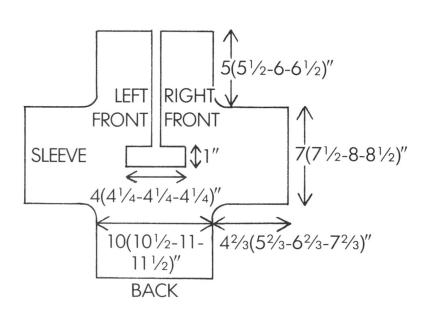

Directions to Follow

Use the directions for making the pullover until you find 2 asterisks (**). At that point continue with these directions.

Next Row: Bind off first 20 (25, 30, 35) sts, work across next 28 (29, 30, 32) sts.

Continue on remaining sts, keeping 4 sts at front edge in garter st, and dec 1 st at arm edge every other row 3 times.

Continue in pattern on remaining sts until front measures same as back from underarm to garter st border.

Work 8 rows in garter st. Bind off.

Complete right side to match left front.

Finishing: With right sides tog, sew sleeve and side seams.

Cord: Attach yarn at one neck edge and work ch sts for 5 ins, using crochet hook. Fasten off. Rep on other neck edge.

Make another pair of ties 2 ins from neck edge. Weave in yarn ends.

Hooded Baby Wrap

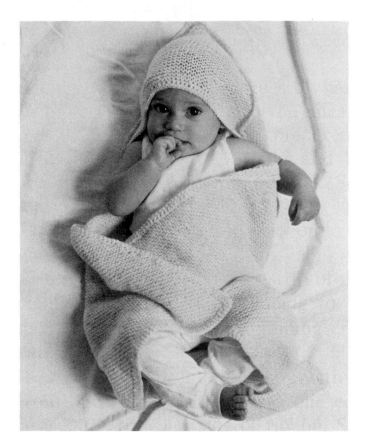

A small triangle gives this pretty blanket a practical touch. The tiny hood provides protection for a baby just out of the bath.

Information to Note

Size: 28 × 28 ins

Materials: 4 pull skeins, 100 grams, Brunswick Windrush®, in desired color

Tools: Circular knitting needle— No. 8 (Canadian No. 5) Stitch holder Crochet hook—No. 8 (H), aluminum

Gauge: 5 sts = 1 inch

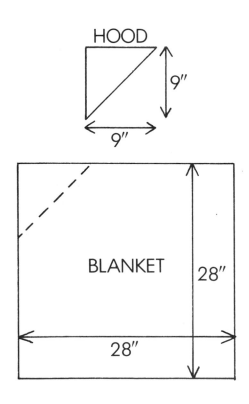

Directions to Follow

Blanket: Begin at corner. Cast on 3 sts. Use circular needle in the same way as regular ones.

Row 1: Inc in 1st st by knitting into front, then back of st. K across to last st inc in last st by same method.

Row 2: K.

Following Rows: Rep last 2 rows until side edge measures 28 ins.

Next Row: K 2 tog, K to last 2 sts, K 2 tog.

Next Row: K. Rep last 2 rows until 3 sts remain. Bind off.

Hood: Work as for blanket until side edge measures 9 ins. Bind off, but do not cut yarn. Use it to crochet edging across long edge. Ch 1, sc into each st. Ch 1, turn sc across. Fasten off.

Edging: Place hood over 1 corner of blanket, matching direction of garter stitch ridges.

Row 1: Attach yarn on side of blanket, ch 1 sc around entire edge of blanket. Working through both layers where hood overlaps blanket and working 3 sc into each corner, sl st to join at end of rnd. Ch 1, sc around sl st to join. Fasten off.

Mittens with Bows

Tiny hands will stay warm and cozy in these easy-to-knit mittens. Ribbing hugs the wrist, and garter stitches cover the hand. Adding a cord and bow gives a pretty touch.

Information to Note

Size: 6 months (1 year)
Material: 1 ball 2-ply baby yarn
Tools: Knitting needles—Size 3
       Crochet hook—Size E
Gauge: 7 sts = 1 inch

Directions to Follow

Cuff: Cast on 34 (38) sts.

Row 1: Working on wrong side, P 2, *K 2, P 2; repeat from * to end of row.

Row 2: K 2, *P 2, K 2; repeat from * to end of row.

Repeat Rows 1 and 2 until ribbing measures 1¾ (2) in from beg. End with Row 1.

Beading: Working on right side, K 2 tog, *yo, K 2 tog; repeat from * to end, leaving 33 (37) sts.

Hand: K each row for garter st until mitten measures 2½ (3) ins from cuff.

First Shaping Row: K 1, *K 2 tog, K 1; repeat from *, end last repeat K 2 tog (K 1) leaving 22 (25) sts on needle.

Next 5 Rows: K.

Second Shaping Row: K 2 tog, 7 (8) times, end K 1; 8 (9) sts remain on needle. Cut yarn, leaving an 18-in end. Draw yarn through all sts, twice. Fasten yarn.

Joining: Sew side edges tog.

Cord: Crochet 97 chain sts. Skip first st, then make a sc in each of the 96 chains, page 41. Fasten yarn. Draw cord through beading. Make knot in each end of cord.

Dainty Booties

A pretty gift for tiny feet—made entirely of garter stitches. The booties are easy and quick to knit.

Information to Note

Size: Infants
Material: 1 ounce Coats & Clark Red Heart® baby yarn
Tools: Knitting needles—No. 4 Tapestry needle
Gauge: 6 sts = 1 inch

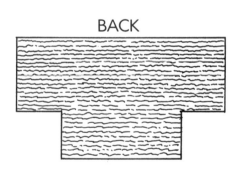

BACK

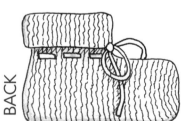

BACK

Directions to Follow

The work begins at the back. Cast on 48 sts. Knit in garter st for 26 rows. Bind off 11 sts at beg of next 2 rows, leaving 26 sts on needle. K 20 rows.

Next Row: Dec 1 st each side, leaving 24 sts on needle.

Following Row: K row even.

Next 2 Rows: K 2 tog across row, leaving 6 sts. Cut yarn. Draw it through the 6 sts. Pull up. Fasten securely, making the toe.

Finishing: Fold bootie in half. Join front and then back, weaving edges together.

Ties: Make 2 twisted cords (page 41), each 16 inches long. Run through bootie at ankle. Tie into bow. Fold down cuff.

Slipper Socks for the Family

Tired and tender feet will find this simple design warm and relaxing. Its flat construction makes it easy and quick to knit. Leave the socks plain for a tailored look, or add a tassel for a decorative touch.

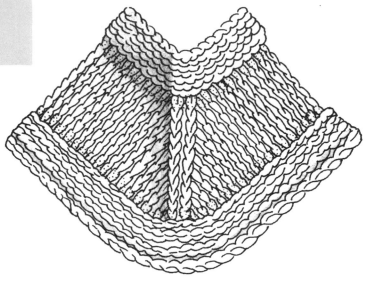

Information to Note

Sizes: Small 7½ inches, (medium 9 inches, large 10 inches)

Material: 2 skeins 4-ply Coats & Clark Red Heart® yarn handknitting yarn

Small amount contrasting color for tassel

Tools: Knitting needles— No. 10½
Tapestry needle

Gauge: 6½ sts = 1 inch

Directions to Follow

Working with 2 strands of yarn, cast on 52 (58, 66) sts.

Bottom. K 8 (10, 10) rows in garter st.

Upper. To start shaping, K 23 (26, 30), P 2 tog. Place marker, K 2, place marker, P 2 tog, K 23 (26, 30) sts to end of row.

Next Row: P 22 (25, 29) sts, K 2 tog, move marker, P 2, move marker, K 2 tog, P 22 (25, 29) sts to end.

Repeat last 2 rows, decreasing before and after the markers until 26 (28, 30) sts remain on needle. Do not dec on last P row.

Top Band. K 6 rows, making 3 ridges of garter sts. Bind off loosely.

Finishing. Sew bottom and back edges tog so the seam is flat.

Tassel Trim. For each sock, cut 2 pieces of yarn about 7 ins long to use as a tie. Then wrap yarn around a 2½-inch piece of cardboard as many times as needed. To hold the strands together, slip 1 of the short pieces of yarn under the wrapped yarn at one end. Tie it securely, drawing the strands tog, slip 1 of the short pieces of yarn under the wrapped yarn at one end. Tie it securely, drawing the strands together. At the other end, cut the yarn (A). Wrap the other short piece of yarn around the tied end twice and tie securely. Trim the ends evenly if necessary. Attach tassel to front at bottom of band.

Pocket Shoulder Bag

It is always handy to have a small bag to dangle from one's neck or shoulder. This one has a pretty textured look and is easy, quick, and inexpensive to knit. You may find it so useful that you will want to make several in different colors.

Information to Note

Size: Approximately 7½ inches
Material: 1 skein rug yarn in desired color
Tools: Knitting needles—No. 5 and No. 10
Crochet hook—Size H
Gauge: 7 sts = 2 inches, using No. 10 needles

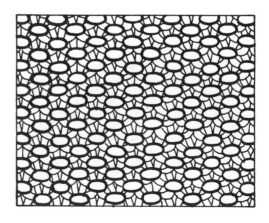

Directions to Follow

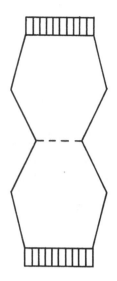

Using the smaller needles, No. 5, cast on 20 sts for the top edge.

Row 1: Work in ribbing—K 1, P 1.

Following Rows: Continue ribbing for 1½ ins.

Next Row: Change to No. 10 needles and begin to knit in *Seed Stitch* pattern. Be sure there are an even number of stitches on needle. To make Seed Stitch, follow this sequence of stitches:

Row 1: *K 1, P 1. Repeat from * across row.

Row 2: *P 1, K 1. Repeat from * across row.

Continue alternating these two rows for 4 ins. Piece should now measure about 5½ ins.

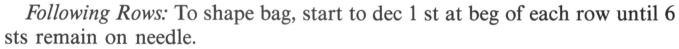

Following Rows: To shape bag, start to dec 1 st at beg of each row until 6 sts remain on needle.

Next 2 Rows: Knit to form ridge.

Following Rows: Working in Seed Stitch, inc 1 st at beg of each row until there are 20 sts on needle. Continue to work even for 4 ins.

Change to No. 5 needles. Work in ribbing of K 1, P 1 for 1½ ins. Bind off. Leave yarn attached so you can crochet the strap with it.

Finishing: Press lightly on wrong side with damp cloth. With wrong sides tog, fold piece in half along ridge.

Attach yarn at top edge. Join edges with sc sts. The hook passes through both layers. Work evenly. Fasten yarn and clip.

For Strap: Using strand of yarn left at top, crochet a chain 34 ins long. Fasten yarn. Sew strap to other side of the bag at the top edge.

Dolman Cardigan

The dolman sleeves add a fashion note to this youthful sweater. With the sleeves knitted in with the back and the front, it becomes a comfortable sweater to wear.

Information to Note

Size: To fit chest/bust: 22 (24, 26, 28, 30) inches

Measurement above Ribbing: 25¾ (29, 30¼, 33¼, 35⅜) inches—buttoned

Materials: 5 (6, 7, 8, 9) balls, 50 grams, Patons Diana No. 9043, Aqua

Buttons 4 (5, 5, 6, 7)

Tools: Circular knitting needles (Susan Bates®)—Sizes 7 and 10 (U.S.), 29 inches

Tapestry needle

Gauge: 15 sts = 4 inches

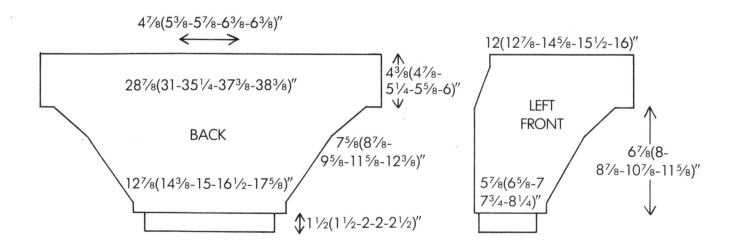

Directions to Follow

Back: With smaller needle, cast on 41 (43, 47, 53, 55) sts. Work back and forth in ribbing as follows:

Row 1 (Right Side): K 1, *P 1, K 1; rep from * across.

Row 2: P 1, *K 1, P 1; rep from * across.

Rep Rows 1 and 2 for 1½ (1½, 2, 2, 2½) ins. On last row, inc 7 (11, 9, 9, 11) sts evenly, end Row 2—48 (54, 56, 62, 66) sts.

Following Rows: Change to larger needle and stockinette st. Beg K row, shaping sides by increasing 1 st each end of 5th row, then every right-side row until there are 64 (80, 76, 100, 112) sts. Work 1 row. Now inc 1 st each end of every row until there are 96 (104, 120, 128, 132) sts, end wrong-side row.

Next 2 Rows: Cast on 6 sts beg of next 2 rows—108 (116, 132, 140, 144) sts. Work even for 22 (24, 26, 28, 30) rows, end wrong-side row. Bind off 45 (48, 55, 58, 60) sts beg of next 2 rows. Put remaining 18 (20, 22, 24, 24) sts on a holder.

Left Front: With smaller needle, cast on 20 (22, 24, 26, 28) sts. Work back and forth in ribbing as follows:

Row 1 (Right Side): K 1, *P 1, K 1; rep from * to last st, K 1.

Row 2: *K 1, P 1; rep from * across.

Rep Rows 1 and 2 for 1½ (1½, 2, 2, 2½) inches. On last row, inc 2 (3, 2, 3, 2) sts evenly, end Row 2—22 (25, 26, 29, 31) sts.

Following Rows: Change to larger needle and stockinette st. Beg K row, shaping side by increasing 1 st at beg of 5th row, then every right-side row until there are 30 (38, 36, 48, 54) sts. Work 1 row. Now inc 1 st at same edge every row until there are 44 (48, 56, 60, 60) sts, end wrong-side row.

Shape Front Slope—Next Row: Inc in 1st st. K to last 2 sts, K 2 tog.

Next Row: P to last 2 sts, inc in next st, P 1.

For Largest Size only—Next Row: Inc in 1st st, K to end.

Next Row: P 2 tog, P to last 2 sts, inc in next st, P 1.

All Sizes: Cast on 6 sts, K to end—51 (55, 63, 67, 68) sts.

Next Row: [P 2 tog] 1 (1, 1, 1, 0) time, P to end.

Continue shaping front slope only by decreasing 1 st every 3rd row from previous dec until 45 (48, 55, 58, 60) sts remain. Work even for 7 (6, 5, 4, 8) more rows, end wrong-side row. Bind off.

Right Front: With smaller needle, cast on 20 (22, 24, 26, 28) sts. Work back and forth in ribbing as follows:

Row 1 (Right Side): K 2, *P 1, K 1; rep from * across.

Row 2: *P 1, K 1; rep from * across.

Complete to correspond to left front, reversing shapings.

Finishing—Cuffs: Sew shoulder and upper sleeve seams. With right sides facing and smaller needle, pick up 23 (25, 27, 29, 31) sts evenly across lower edge of sleeve. Do not join. Work back and forth in ribbing in same way as for back, for 1½ (1½, 2, 2, 2½) ins, beg Row 2, end wrong-side row. Bind off loosely in rib, using larger needle. Sew cuff, lower sleeve, and side seams.

Front Bands: With right sides facing and smaller needle, pick up 31 (36, 41, 48, 51) sts from lower right edge to beg of front slope shaping, 24 (26, 28, 28, 31) sts to shoulder, K across 18 (20, 22, 24, 24) sts of back, dec 1 st, pick up 24 (26, 28, 28, 31) sts along left front to beg of slope shaping, and 31 (36, 41, 48, 51) sts to lower edge—127 (143, 159, 175, 187) sts. Work back and forth in ribbing as follows:

Row 1 (Wrong Side): K 1, *P 1, K 1; rep from * across.

Row 2: K 2, *P 1, K 1; rep from * to last st, K 1.

Work 1 more row in ribbing.

Buttonhole Row: Rib 3 (2, 3, 3, 2), [bind off 2 sts, rib 6 including st on needle after bind-off] 4 (5, 5, 6, 7) times, rib to end.

Next Row: [Rib to bind off, turn, cast on 2 sts, turn] 4 (5, 5, 6, 7) times, rib to end.

Rib 2 more rows. Bind off loosely in rib, using larger needle. Sew on buttons.

A Pretty Cloth

One doesn't usually think of a dishcloth as being pretty, but this one is. The bias effect of the garter stitches and the eyelet border detail create an interesting effect. The square is so soft that it could be used as a facecloth.

Information to Note

Size: Approximately 8 × 8 inches
Materials: 1 ball, 2.5 ounces,
    100% cotton yarn
Tool: Knitting needles—No. 9
Gauge: 4 sts = 1 inch

Directions to Follow

Cast on 4 sts.
Row 1 (inc): K 2, yo, K across row.
Row 2: Rep Row 1, making increases until there are 44 sts on needles.
Next Row (dec): K 1, K 2 tog, yo, K 2 tog. K to end of row.
Following Rows: Repeat previous row until 4 sts remain on needle.
Bind off. Cut yarn and fasten, weaving ends into cloth.

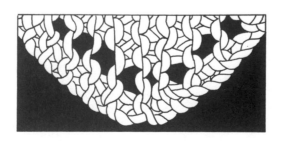

Dog's Turtleneck

A smart and comfy coat for your pet has front slits for the front legs. This feature makes it easier to dress your dog.

Information to Note

Sizes: Small (Medium, Large)
　　　Neck to base of tail 12 (14, 16) inches
　　　Girth 14 (16, 18) inches
Materials: 4 (6, 8) ounces knitting worsted
Tools: Knitting needles—No. 6 and No. 7
　　　Steel crochet hook—No. 00
Gauge: 6 sts = 1 inch

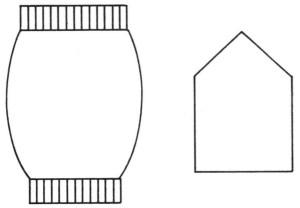

Directions to Follow

Back: Beginning at neck edge, cast on 46 (58, 70) sts, using No. 6 needles.
　Row 1: K 2, *P 2, K 2. Rep from * across row.
　Row 2: P 2, *K 2, P 2. Rep from * across row.
　Repeat rows 1 and 2 for 3 ins, ending with a Row 2. When you are knitting this row, add 3 sts so there will be 49 (61, 73) sts on needle. Be sure to add the sts at even intervals. Change to No. 7 needles and knit as follows:
　Next Row (Right Side): K 1, *P 1, K 1. Rep from * across row.
　Following Row: P 1, *K 1, P 1. Rep from * across row.
　Rep these 2 rows.

As you inc 1 st at beg and end of every other row 5 (6, 7) times, be sure to continue the ribbing in an unbroken line. Do this until there are 59 (73, 87) sts on needle.

Work evenly until piece measures 13 (14, 15) ins. End with a wrong-side row and 1 (3, 1) sts on last row.

Change to No. 6 needles. Work in K 2, P 2 ribbing for 10 rows. Bind off loosely in ribbing.

Under-panel: Cast on 3 sts, using No. 7 needles. Work in ribbing, K 1, P 1 across row. At the beg and end of every row inc 1 st for 12 (13, 14) times. Work even on 27 (29, 31) sts until panel measures 5 ins from beg.

Next Row: Dec 1 st at beg and end.

Following Rows: Continue to dec 1 st at beg and end of every 4th row. Do this 4 times. Work even on 17 (19, 21) sts until piece measures 7 ins. Bind off.

Joining Parts: Sew turtleneck ribbing together. Then join under-panel to back along increased edges. Leaving 2½ ins open for legs, sew decreased edges of under-panel to back.

Finishing: Crochet 1 row of sc around each leg opening.

"Block at a Time" Afghan

Working in blocks makes this afghan an easy one to handle as you knit. Variations in color plus the diagonal arrangement of the garter stitches creates an interesting design pattern.

Information to Note

Size: 44 × 55 inches

Materials: 12 ounces each of 4 colors of your choice. This afghan was made of No. 356, Taupe; No. 255, Burnt Orange; No. 245, Orange; and No. 602, Dark Gold, using Coats & Clark Red Heart® 4-ply hand knitting yarn, Art. E. 267

Tools: Knitting needles—No. 8 Tapestry needle

Gauge: 4 sts = 1 inch Each block measures 5½ inches square

Directions to Follow

First Block (Make 20): With Dark Gold, cast on 1 st, turn.

Row 1: K in front and in back of 1st st—1 st inc.

Row 2: K 1, inc 1 st in last st—3 sts.

Row 3: K to last st, inc 1 st in last st.

Rows 4–33: Repeat Row 3. There are 24 sts on last row and half of the block has been made. Break off yarn and attach yarn (Orange) for second half of block.

Row 34: Insert needle through back of first 2 sts, K 2 tog; *yo, K tog through back of next 2 sts. Rep from * across—33 sts.

Row 35: K to last 2 sts, K 2 tog.

Rows 36–66: Rep Row 35. One st remains on last row. Break off and draw end through remaining st.

Second Block (Make 20): Work as for first block, using Dark Gold for Rows 1–33 and Burnt Orange for Rows 34–66.

Third Block (Make 20): Work as for first block, using Taupe for Rows 1–33 and Burnt Orange for Rows 34–66.

Fourth Block (Make 20): Work as for first block, using Taupe for Rows 1–33 and Orange for Rows 34–66.

Joining: Following Diagram A for position of colors and direction of rows, sew a first, second, third, and fourth block together to form a larger square. Sew 19 more squares in the same way; sew squares together as indicated in Diagram B.

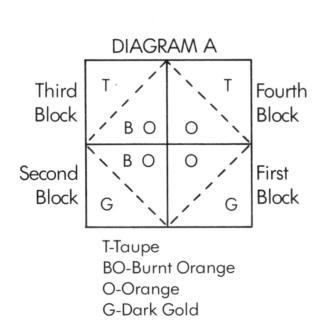

DIAGRAM A

Third Block

Fourth Block

Second Block

First Block

T-Taupe
BO-Burnt Orange
O-Orange
G-Dark Gold

DIAGRAM B

3	4	3	4	3	4	3	4
2	1	2	1	2	1	2	1
3	4	3	4	3	4	3	4
2	1	2	1	2	1	2	1
3	4	3	4	3	4	3	4
2	1	2	1	2	1	2	1
3	4	3	4	3	4	3	4
2	1	2	1	2	1	2	1
3	4	3	4	3	4	3	4
2	1	2	1	2	1	2	1

1-First Block
2-Second Block
3-Third Block
4-Fourth Block

The Useful Stole

A stole is a fashion item that is always nice to have. This one made with garter stitches alternating with dropped ones is quick and easy to knit.

Information to Note

Size: 73 inches long and 20 inches wide, excluding fringe

Material: 7 skeins 2-ply Coats & Clark Red Heart® sport yarn, Art. E. 281

Tool: Knitting needles—No. 11

Gauge: 3 sts = 1 inch

GARTER

DROPPED STITCHES

Directions to Follow

Starting at narrow edge with 2 strands held tog, cast on 66 sts.

Rows 1–4: Knit.

Row 5: K 1, *yo, K 1. Repeat from * across.

Row 6: K 1, *drop next yo, K 1. Repeat from * across—66 sts.

Repeat these 6 rows for pattern until total length is 73 ins. End with Row 4. Bind off loosely.

Fringe: Cut 3 strands of yarn each 12 ins long. Double these strands to form a loop. Insert a crochet hook in 1st st of one narrow edge and draw loop through. Draw loose ends through loop and pull up tightly to form a knot. Knot 3 strands as before in each st across. Work fringe along opposite narrow edge in same way. Trim fringe evenly.

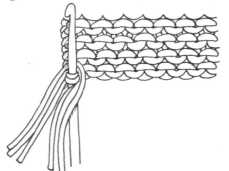 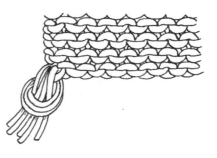

Bloused Pullover

Eyelets at the waistline allows this classic sweater to be bloused. This creates a soft effect, which can be very flattering.

Information to Note

Size: 10 (12, 14, 16, 18)
   Finished chest measurements: 34 (36, 38, 40, 42) inches
Materials: 9 (10, 11, 12, 13) balls, 40 grams, Brunswick Thistledown
Tools: Knitting needles No. 8 (Canadian knitting needles No. 7 and No. 5) Circular knitting needles— No. 6 Crochet hook No. 8 (H), aluminum Holder Tapestry needle
Gauge: 4 sts = 1 inch

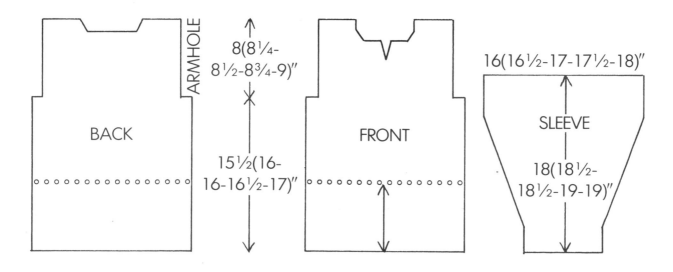

Directions to Follow

Back: With larger needles, cast on 69 (73, 77, 81, 85) sts and work K 1, P 1 ribbing as follows:

Row 1: K 1, *P 1, K 1; rep from *.

Row 2: P 1, *K 1, P 1; rep from *. Rep Rows 1 and 2 for 7 ins.

Eyelet Row (Right-Side Row): K 1, *yo, K 2 tog; rep from * across. Change to stockinette st and dec 1 st in 1st row, then work even until piece measures 15½ (16, 16, 16½, 17) ins from beg or desired length to under-arm.

Shape Armholes: Bind off 5 sts at beg of next 2 rows. Work even on remaining 58 (62, 66, 70, 74) sts until armholes measures 7 (7¼, 7½, 7¾, 8) ins.

Shape Back Neck: Work across 24 (25, 26, 27, 29) sts, place next 10 (12, 14, 16, 16) sts on holder for back of neck, with another skein work across last 24 (25, 26, 27, 29) sts. Working each side separately, dec 1 st at neck edge of next 5 rows. Bind off each shoulder—19 (20, 21, 22, 24) sts.

Front: Work same as back to armholes.

Shape Front Armholes: Bind off 5 sts at beg of next 2 rows. Work even on remaining 58 (62, 66, 70, 74) sts until armhole measures 3 ins.

Divide for Slit: K across 29 (31, 33, 35, 37) sts; with another skein K to end. Working each side separately, keeping 1 st on each side of neck slit in garter st and all other sts in stockinette st, work even until armholes measures 5 (5¼, 5½, 5¾, 6) ins, ending with a P row.

Shape Left Front Neck: Knit across 26 (27, 28, 29, 31) sts, place next 3 (4, 5, 6, 6) sts on holder for front neck, then dec 1 st at neck edge of every row 3 times, then every other row 4 times more. Work even until armhole measures same as back. Bind off shoulder.

Shape Right Front Neck: Reversing shaping, work right front to match left front neck.

Sleeves: With smaller needles, cast on 28 (30, 32, 32, 34) sts. Work K 1, P 1 ribbing for 3 ins, inc 14 sts in last row—42 (44, 46, 46, 48) sts. Change to larger needles and stockinette st and inc 1 st each side of every 6th row until there are 64 (66, 68, 70, 72) sts on needle. Work even until sleeve measures 18 (18½, 18½, 19, 19) ins, or 1 in more than desired length to underarm. Bind off.

Finishing: Weave shoulder seams. Sew sleeve into armhole, matching center of sleeve to top of shoulder seam and 1 in of side of sleeve to the 5 bound-off sts of back and front of armhole. Weave side and sleeve seams.

Neckband: From right side, with smaller circular needles, pick up 1 st in each st around entire neck, beginning at center front and including sts from holders; dec 1 st if necessary to make an odd number of sts.

Eyelet Row: K 1, *yo, K 2 tog; rep from * around neck. Bind off in P sts.

Belt and Neck Cord: Using double yarn and crochet hook, make a ch 46 (48, 50, 52, 54) ins for belt and another 34 (34, 36, 36, 38) ins for neck cord. Thread through eyelets, beginning at center front.

A Wrap Cardigan

Brunswick Yarns

The surprise feature of this cardigan is a draped collar that can be used as a hood. The belted wrap and the hood make this sweater a handy one to have in your wardrobe.

Information to Note

Size: 10 (12, 14, 16, 18)
   Finished chest measurement 34 (36, 38, 40, 42) inches

Materials: 7 (7, 8, 8, 9) pull skeins, 100 grams, Brunswick Germantown Knitting Worsted

Tools: Circular knitting needle— No. 8 (Canadian needle No. 5)
   Stitch holder
   Tapestry needle

Gauge: 5 sts = 1 inch

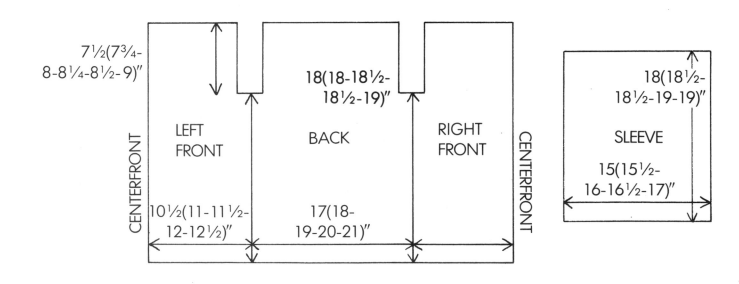

7½(7¾-8-8¼-8½-9)″

18(18-18½-18½-19)″

LEFT FRONT

BACK

RIGHT FRONT

CENTERFRONT

CENTERFRONT

10½(11-11½-12-12½)″

17(18-19-20-21)″

18(18½-18½-19-19)″

SLEEVE

15(15½-16-16½-17)″

Directions to Follow

The directions will be easier to use if you check your position as you knit.

Body. Knit in one piece to underarm. With circular needle, cast on 190 (200, 210, 220, 230) sts and work in garter st for 2 ins.

Next Row (Wrong Side): K 10, P across to within 10 sts of end, K 10.

Following Row: K. Rep last 2 rows until piece measures from beg 18 (18, 18½, 18½, 19) ins, ending with a wrong-side row.

Divide for Armhole: K across 48 (50, 52, 55, 57) sts for right front, place next 84 (90, 96, 100, 106) sts on holder for right underarm and back, place remaining 58 (60, 62, 65, 67) sts on holder for left underarm and front.

Right Front: Working on the sts of right front only, P across to last 10 sts, K 10. Keeping the 10 sts at front edge in garter st and all other sts in stockinette st, work even on 48 (50, 52, 55, 57) sts until armhole measures 7½ (7¾, 8, 8¼, 8½) ins, ending with a wrong-side row. Place first 23 sts on holder for front of hood. Bind off remaining 25 (27, 29, 32, 34) sts for shoulder.

Back: From right side of work, attach yarn and bind off first 10 sts from holder, then K the 74 (80, 86, 90, 96) remaining sts of back. Work even in stockinette st until armholes measure same as right front armhole. Bind off 25 (27, 29, 32, 34) sts at beg next 2 rows. Place remaining 24 (26, 28, 26, 28) sts on holder for back of hood.

Left Front: From right side of work, attach yarn and bind off first 10 sts from left front holder for underarm, then K remaining 48 (50, 52, 55, 57) sts from holder. Keeping the 10 sts at front edge in garter st and all other sts in stockinette st, work even until armhole measures same as right front, ending with wrong-side row. Bind off first 25 (27, 29, 32, 34) sts for shoulder, then place remaining 23 sts on holder for front of hood.

Sleeves: Cast on 75 (77, 80, 82, 85) sts and work in garter st for 2 ins. Change to stockinette st and work even until sleeve measures 16 (16½, 16½, 17, 17) ins. Change to garter st and work 2 more ins. Bind off.

Finishing: Backstitch shoulder seams. Fold sleeve tog with seam edges even. Insert the bound-off edge of top of sleeve into the armhole, centering top of sleeve at shoulder seam. Sew all of top of sleeve to straight edge of armhole. Stitch the bound-off sts of underarm to the side seam of the sleeve on each side. Weave the remaining sleeve seam tog.

Hood: Using circular needle, from right side pick up and K sts from right front holder, back holder, and left front holder.

Row 1 (Wrong Side): K 10, P across to last 10 sts, K 10.

Row 2: K 10, inc every 6th st, K around to last 10 sts, K 10.

Row 3: Same as Row 1.

Row 4: K. Rep rows 3 and 4 until hood measures 14 ins. Bind off. Fold hood and backstitch seam in top of hood.

Belt: Cast on 8 sts and work even in garter st until belt measures 48 (50, 52, 54, 56) ins or desired length. Bind off.

PART III

Quilting

Notes

If you like variety, then you will surely like quilting. It offers so many possibilities for decorative needlework, not only in the types of quilting, but also in how and where it can be used. Although one usually thinks of quilting in connection with quilt making, it actually has become a fashion item. It is often used as a decorative touch for many household and personal articles, ranging from a pillow to a bag.

Quilting can be done by hand and machine. Today a combination of both is often seen, with the hand quilting being used for the visible part and the machine for the underneath construction. Quilting can also be combined with appliqué, embroidery, and patchwork to create various effects.

The Different Look

Quilting began by decorating a plain-colored fabric with tiny stitches for a whole-cloth quilt. At first the lines were straight, forming geometric designs. Gradually the lines began to curve. Designs continued to grow more elaborate, featuring scallops, feathers, birds, and flowers. Sometimes the stitches were arranged to tell a story. When appliqué began to be used for a utilitarian patch, the quilting stitches began to play a supporting role.

Finally some inventive women decided to sew bits of material together to create a bigger piece of material instead of adding a patch to worn fabric. This lead to the introduction of the patchwork design. Putting the pieces together was called piecing. One pieced a quilt.

The Basic Techniques

Quilting is actually a form of sewing. The same techniques are used for both. If you know how to sew, you will have no difficulty with quilting.

The Composition. For quilting, 3 layers of material are usually employed and held together with running or quilting stitches. There is the decorative top, a soft filler, and a backing.

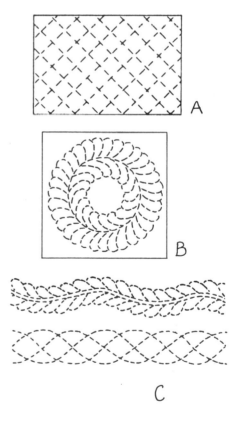

Before putting the layers together, the design for the top should be determined. This will influence the quilting pattern. It can be an allover design (A) or just an outline. Or it can be a motif (B) in a block between patchwork squares or for a border (C). But whatever type of quilting you are going to do, you should transfer the design to the top before beginning to work.

The transferring of the design can be done in various ways. A pencil marking, using a no. 2 pencil, or an artist's chalk pencil is most often used. The line should be lightly drawn, using a ruler, template, or stencil. You want to be sure the line can be removed by washing.

Increasing or decreasing the size of the design to fit the area into which it is to be placed is necessary. By drawing a grid of accurately placed horizontal and vertical lines, this can be done without too much trouble. The sizes of the squares can vary from ⅛ inch for a small design to 1 inch for a larger one.

After deciding on the size of the finished design, draw a grid on another piece of paper with the lines the correct distance apart. For instance, if you want to double the pattern and the original lines were ½ inch apart, the new grid would be made with lines 1 inch apart. Copy the design outline on the graph paper, transferring it from the smaller squares to correspond to the larger ones.

Assembling. After the top layer has been prepared, you can put the layers together. The top can just be marked with the quilting design, or it can be a finished decorative piece if you are using patchwork or appliqué. Begin with the *backing.* Place it wrong side up on a flat surface. Smooth it out and then add the *batting,* the second layer. Smooth it out evenly so the thickness of the batting is even throughout. Follow with the *top.* Be sure the right side is up. Beginning at the center, smooth it out. Usually the edges are kept together.

Basting. The 3 layers are held together with basting stitches. Although the stitches are temporary, they should be made very carefully so the layers remain securely together. Basting from the center to the sides and corners in a sunburst effect works nicely.

Hand Quilting. An easy-to-make running stitch is used. Although it is a simple sewing stitch, it seems to appear different. Probably it is because the stitches are made with precision, each stitch short and even. Today the stitches are larger than those found on antique quilts. Five to 8 stitches on the top side are considered attractive.

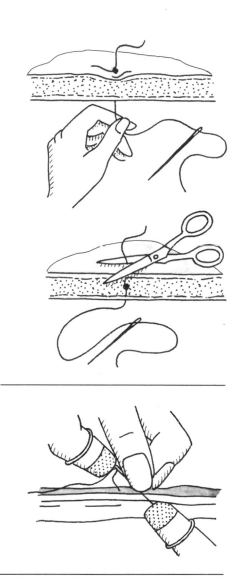

Making the stitch can be done in 2 ways. You can decide which you prefer. One stitch can be made at a time or 2 or 3 stitches can be taken by weaving the needle in and out. Use a thread no longer than 18 inches. Knot one end. Start at the middle of the design and work outward. Gently but firmly pull the thread through the top layer so the knot becomes embedded in the batting. Continue to push the needle through the backing. Be sure to protect your finger with a thimble. In fact, quilters often use a thimble on both hands, not only to protect the fingers but also to help regulate the size and placement of the stitches.

Ending a row of stitches needs a backstitch. After making it, pull the thread taut. Then, for security, move the needle and thread through the stitch and into the batting. Push the needle through the batting for about ¾ inch. Bring it up on the quilting line. Clip the thread close to the fabric.

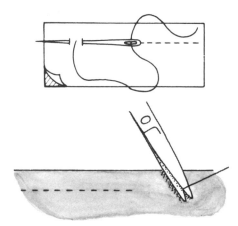

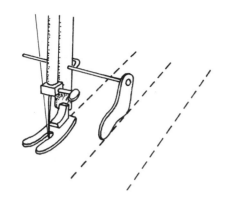

Machine Quilting. Although hand quilting has an heirloom quality that machine quilting doesn't have, more and more machine quilting is used. It works best for smaller areas that are easy to handle. By using a special attachment, straight lines can be stitched quickly and easily. If the quilting seems difficult to handle, roll the piece up so it fits under the arm. As you stitch, smooth out the work as it moves under the presser foot. Stitch from the center to the edge. Be careful that tucks do not appear where the stitching lines cross.

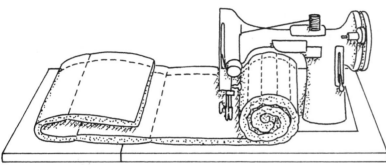

Some Needed Supplies

In contrast to the few tools that crocheting and knitting require, quilting seems to need a lot. Although many are available, the number can be kept to a minimum—needle and thread. It all depends on your personal preferences.

For sewing, many of the items will be found among your sewing supplies—thread, needle, pins, pincushion, and thimble, as well as scissors and shears.

There is a special quilting thread. If you can't find it in your area, use a good, all-purpose thread, no. 50. For basting, a strong thread is needed to hold the pieces together as they are stretched in the hoop and folded and unfolded.

Matching thread is usually used for sewing, whereas white is more often seen in quilting. Sometimes a color that blends or contrasts with the top is preferred.

There is also a special needle for quilting known as a "between." It is shorter than the needles usually used for sewing, such as sharps and embroidering or crewel, which are longer and more slender. The shorter needle seems to make it easier to produce tiny stitches. For quilting and sewing, size 8 seems to be a good one.

For other activities, such as *marking,* there are the hard pencils or marking pen and ruler. For *designing,* templates, graph paper, cardboard, dressmaker's carbon, and plastic sheets are available. You may want to experiment before you select any of these products.

Hoops and *frames* are devices that make it easier to perfect quilting stitches by holding the fabric taut. This is especially so when standing ones are employed, allowing both hands to work freely.

In the beginning the frame was large, in order to accommodate a big quilt and allow several women to quilt at the same time. Frames are still available, but probably hoops are more frequently used today. They are made in a variety of sizes to suit projects of various sizes. A round one is best.

The Fabric. Almost any type of fabric can be quilted. It all depends on what you are making. In the early days of quilting in this country, the ragbag provided many of the materials. Today new fabrics are usually used, and they are not always easy to find. But whatever you select, remember to keep the material for the 3 layers appropriate for one another.

For the *top layer,* which is the display side, choose a fabric in the best quality you can afford. It should be light to medium in weight, opaque so the seams won't show, and easy for the needle to move. A 100 percent cotton broadcloth, percale, calico, chambray, and muslin are usually suitable. If a cotton blend is being used, then it is best to construct the complete project out of material of the same content. Testing it for color fastness, shrinkage, and pressing before using it is a good idea.

For the *backing or bottom layer,* try a material similar to the top in type, quality, and style, but perhaps not quite as decorative. Although a patterned material can be used, a plain one is often preferred. A sheet provides a good backing, eliminating seams.

For the inner layer, which is sandwiched between the top and bottom ones, a variety of fillers can be employed. Batting of various fibers, cotton flannel, or even a blanket is a possibility. Although the filling adds warmth, it also provides a three-dimensional effect, creating a certain beauty in the work. The degree of puffiness you desire will influence the type of filling you choose. Cotton flannel gives a flat effect, whereas batting can create a light, fluffy one. Today batting is available in different degrees of loft.

Batting is purchased in batts of various sizes. If the project is large, you may have to join 2 batts to obtain the needed size. Keeping a record of the effect you obtained by quilting with certain battings will simplify future work.

Designs for Quilting

In order to give you some idea of the number of ways quilting can be utilized to provide a decorative touch, a variety of articles are shown on the following pages. Although suggestions are given on how to interpret the designs, it is hoped that they will inspire you to create your own version. From the smaller designs, larger ones can emerge. The little quilt becomes a larger one; the pillow, a wall hanging; the patchwork stocking block, a lap robe. Choosing colors, fabrics, and uses can give the satisfying feeling of creating your own design.

A Rosy Picture

An interesting way to begin a quilting experience is to use quilting stitches to give depth to a beautiful print. It is easy to do and lovely to see. The resulting puffy effect adds a new dimension.

Information to Note

Size: Any appropriate size can be selected; for this picture, a piece of fabric 12 × 9½ inches was used

Materials: Although a decorator's fabric is usually chosen, it is possible to find a suitable design in other ways. A napkin provided this rose. In selecting a print, look for one in the correct size and color with a plain area around it, and with design details that can be defined with stitches to produce a realistic look.
Thread—in a color that blends with the design
Batting—small piece 12 × 9½ inches
Backing Material—small piece of muslin, 12 × 9½ inches
Frame and mat—select an appropriate size of the shadow-box type so the round protuberance of the design will not be flattened

Tools: Needle, pins, and hoop

Directions to Follow

Cut out piece for top, centering the design, and pieces for backing and batting.

Assemble the 3 layers. Pin and baste together.

Decide which of the design lines to outline. Remember to leave space between lines of stitches so the fabric puffs up. If you wish, place work in frame.

Then, beginning at the center, use small running stitches, regularly spaced, to outline the design. Work toward the outer edges. Gradually the area between the lines will puff up.

When it is completed, put the quilted picture in an appropriate frame.

Teddy to Quilt

At some time nearly everyone has a favorite teddy bear. Here is one with a different look that is easy to quilt and easy to make. By using fabric printed in a patchwork design, the time-consuming task of sewing pieces together is eliminated. All parts of the bear are cut in a single piece.

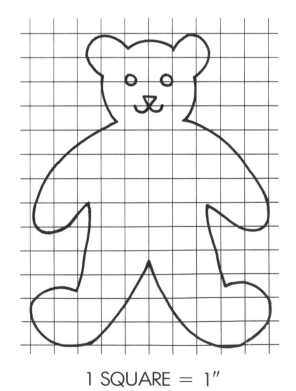

1 SQUARE = 1"

Information to Note

Size: The design shown here is about 13 inches tall; it can be made larger or smaller if you would like to change the size

Materials: 1/2 yard printed fabric
1/4 yard muslin for backing
Batting for stuffing
Black floss for embroidery
2/3 yard ribbon, 1/2 inch wide
Thread, in a blending color

Directions to Follow

Prepare quilted material by cutting 2 rectangles of printed material 16 ✕ 12 inches. Also cut 2 rectangles each of muslin and of batting.

Assemble layers of batting and backing material by basting them to wrong side of the top piece. Machine-quilt the layers together, stitching diagonally across piece 1½ inches apart.

With the quilted material prepared, enlarge the pattern shown here.

Pin pattern to material. Cut out, leaving a ¼-inch seam allowance.

Mark the places on front piece for eyes, nose, and mouth. Embroider eyes and nose in *satin stitches* and the mouth in *outline stitches.*

Place right sides of front and back pieces together. Baste. Stitch a ¼-inch seam around bear, leaving an opening on one side. Press seam.

Turn inside out. Run fingers along seam, smoothing and shaping.

Stuff with batting to give it the desired firmness. Close opening with *overhand stitches.*

Stitch at base of ears, rounding the shape of the head.

Finish with a ribbon tied in a bow around the neck.

In case you do not wish to use machine stitching, the work can be done by hand.

Pretty Place Mat

For a cool, refreshing table setting, this place mat offers the perfect look. The gingham creates a dainty effect and is at the same time easy to work with. The lines provide a perfect guide for quilting. If you add a touch of lace, the feeling becomes even more lighthearted. Of course, other types of fabric can be used for this mat.

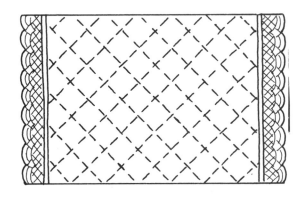

Information to Note

Size: 17 × 12 inches
Materials: ¾ yard gingham or other fabric of your choice
2 yards narrow lace
Batting
Thread in matching color

Directions to Follow

Cut 2 rectangles each 17½ × 12½ inches—1 for the top and 1 for the back.

Cut 2 bias strips 2½ × 12½ inches.

Cut a piece of batting 17 × 12 inches.

Pin batting to wrong side of top piece. Baste in place, leaving a ¼-inch margin around edge. With right sides of fabric together, join back to top piece. Baste in place.

Stitch pieces together with batting side up, leaving an opening on lower edge for turning. Before stitching, place a strip of tissue paper on seam line. When stitching is completed, tear away tissue paper. Press stitching line.

Turn mat inside out. Adjust corners. Baste around edge in order to keep stitching line on edge. Slip-stitch opening together. Press.

To quilt the mat, stitch diagonally across it, using the checks as a guiding line. Keep the rows about 1¼ inches apart.

To make the decorative bands, fold under the raw edges of the bias strips ¼ inch. Cut 4 pieces of lace 18 inches long. Gather lace to fit band. Baste to each side of strips.

Baste lace-trimmed bands to ends of mat. Stitch close to folded edges. Slip-stitch ends of bands to mat.

Eyeglass Case— Single and Double

As glasses have become larger, it has become more difficult to find a case to carry them in. And if you need to carry two pairs, your problem is twofold. To alleviate such a situation, these cases have been designed. The same pattern can be used for a single as well as the double case. By decorating it with a touch of quilting and sewing it in a bright fabric makes it an attractive and easy to find bag accessory.

Information to Note

Size: About 7 × 4 inches

Materials: For outside, a piece of fabric 12 × 10 inches; for lining, a piece of fabric in contrasting color 12 × 10 inches; for backing, a piece of muslin, 12 × 10 inches
Batting
Thread in a matching or blending color

Directions to Follow

Increase size of pattern shown here until design measures 7¾ × 8¼ inches.

Transfer outline of pattern and quilting design to the backing piece.

Place batting on the wrong side of the outside piece, centering it. Cover with the backing piece. Be sure the design is on the outside. Baste the 3 layers together.

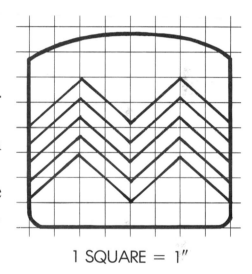

1 SQUARE = 1″

For the decorative quilting, stitch on the design lines that you traced on the backing.

Pin pattern to quilted fabric. Be sure design is placed accurately. Cut out case.

With right sides together, stitch a ¼-inch seam along lower and side edges. Press seam line.

Turn case inside out. Run fingers along seam line to arrange corners. Fold under the upper edge for ¼ inch and baste.

To make the lining, after cutting it out using pattern, put the right sides together and stitch a ¼-inch seam along lower and side edges. Press. Fold the upper edge to the wrong side ¼ inch and baste.

Turn inside out and tuck inside case. Slip-stitch the lining to the outside case along folded edge.

With a few exceptions the case is made in the same way. However, no lining is used. Instead, 2 outside pieces are sewn together to make 2 pockets.

Information to Note

Size: About 7 × 8 inches
Materials: ¼ yard plain fabric;
   ¼ yard printed fabric
   ¼ yard muslin for backing
   Batting
   Thread in a blending color

Directions to Follow

Cut 2 pieces of plain, 2 of printed, and 2 of backing fabrics, each 10 × 12 inches. Transfer outline and zigzag design on backing pieces.

Prepare layers for quilting. After quilting is completed, join the matching lining to it, right sides together. Stitch around the piece, making a ¼-inch seam, leaving an opening on lower edge for turning. Press seam line.

Turn to right side. Baste along outer edges. Slip-stitch opening together.

Place the 2 finished pieces together with the quilting side out. Baste together.

Stitch a center line in order to make 2 pockets. Then stitch on edge along sides, and lower edge, holding the 2 pieces together.

Craft Bag

A bag to keep needed needlework supplies is handy to have. One that can be made easily and inexpensively and still be attractive is especially desirable. Strip quilting is used to make this distinctive fabric.

Information to Note

Size: Finished tote about 16 × 10½ inches

Materials: Scraps of material can be used in 3 different colors, or ¼ yard of each in colors of your choice—brown, cinnamon, and beige were used here.

½ yard backing fabric
Batting
¾ yard lining material in a color of your choice—brown was used for the bag shown here
Thread in a blending color
1 yard cord for handle

Directions to Follow

Cut strips 2¼ inches wide. You will need about 2 yards of each color.

Cut rectangle 22 × 17 inches for backing and a batting piece 21 × 16 inches.

Center batting on backing piece, leaving a ½-inch allowance around the edges. Baste.

Cut a square 2½ × 2½ inches and from it a triangle in color 1. Baste to upper left-hand corner on batting side of backing.

To start the strip quilting, pin a strip, right sides together, to triangle. Stitch through 3 layers (A). Then turn strip over backing and smooth out carefully. Pin strip in place (B). Add the next strip in this way and continue until backing piece is covered, alternating the colors as shown in C.

When piece is completed, fold piece in half, right sides together. Stitch ½-inch seams along side edges. Turn top edge to wrong side ½ inch and baste.

To make lining, cut piece 22 × 17 inches. Also cut piece 12 × 17 inches for lining pockets. On pocket section fold a ¾-inch hem along one long edge. Press and stitch. Then fold piece in half. Press.

Fold lining piece in half, right sides together, and press. Place smaller piece on top, right sides together. Stitch along folded line, making a ½-inch seam. Pin to lining with the hem about 1 inch from top. Then make 2 pockets by stitching on fold line in center of piece (D).

Finish lining by folding it in half. Stitch ½-inch side seams through the 3 layers. Fold under raw edges ½ inch and baste.

To make handles, cut 2 strips 12 × 1½ inches of the darker color and 2 pieces of cord 24 inches long, or twice as long as the handle. Fasten one end of the strip to the center of the cord. Fold strip over cord, wrong sides outward. Stitch close to the cord. Trim seam. Pull the

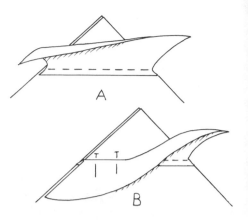

A

B

C

D

encased cord out of the tubing. The strip is auto-matically turned to the right side. The free cord is pulled into the tubing. Cut off the extra cord (E).

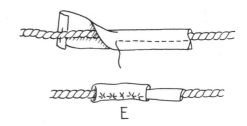

Sew handles to quilted piece about 5 inches from outer edges. Slip-stitch lining to bag along upper edge.

Cushion in Stripes

Strip quilting is one of the easiest and most effective ways to create a pieced fabric. Strips of any color, width, and length can be sewed together to produce a variegated band. In this instance, 8 colors were used to form 2 bands, which were then combined in a patchwork design—a variation of the Roman Square.

Information to Note

Size: Cushion—14 × 14 inches

Materials: Scraps of fabrics in 8 different colors can be used, or 1/8 yard of each new material. The color scheme used for this cushion was for first band coral (1), brown (2), yellow (3), beige (4), and for the second band blue (5), turquoise (6), green (7), gray (8). Combining colors is fun, so you may want to plan another scheme.

Directions to Follow

For the front or top, mark each fabric for strips 15 × 2½ inches. Be sure marking is straight and on grain. Cut strips, being careful to keep edges even.

Make 2 bands, arranging 4 colors in correct sequence as shown (A). Join with ¼-inch seams. Repeat the process with the other colors.

Cut bands in half so you have 4 squares 7½ × 7½ inches.

Arrange squares as shown here (B). Sew squares together with ¼-inch seams. Press.

For quilted effect, cut a square of muslin, 14½ × 14½ inches, and a square of batting, 14 × 14 inches.

Place batting on wrong side of top and then the backing on top. Baste the layers together. Quilt by stitching in the well between each stripe.

For the back, cut 2 sections—one 14½ × 7½ inches, the other 14½ × 12¼ inches. This type of back allows the pillow form to be inserted and removed easily, since it is made in 2 parts.

Make a hem along one of the longer edges of each piece. Fold under the raw edges ¼ inch and then ¾ inch. Press and stitch along folded edge.

With right sides together, place upper or smaller section of back on front, and then the lower section. Stitch around square ¼ inch from edge. Clip across corner. Press seams.

Turn the cover inside out (C). Smooth out, adjusting corners. Insert pillow.

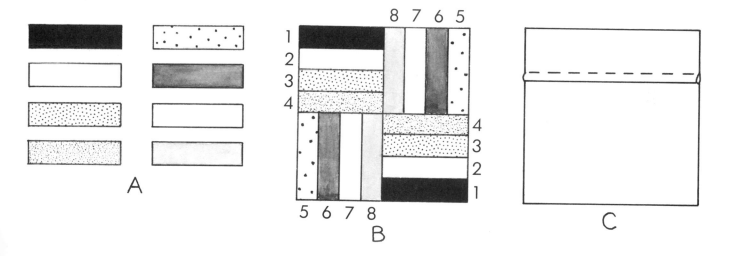

Festive Stocking

Patchwork quilting adds a joyous touch to a Christmas stocking. This one can be made from an old quilt or of newly quilted blocks, using a traditional pattern in a colorful way. For this one, a variation of the 4-Patch block was used in a combination of red, white, and green.

Information to Note

Size: About 18 × 10 inches, using blocks 8 × 8 inches

Materials: 1 yard muslin, 1/4 yard red fabric, 1/4 yard green fabric

Batting

1 yard red ribbon 1 inch wide; 6 inches narrow ribbon

2/3 yard ruffled ecru lace, 1 inch wide

Thread in a blending color

Directions to Follow

To make 4 blocks, use design shown here (A). Cut template 2¼ × 2¼ inches square. Mark fabric. Cut 4 green squares, 6 red, and 6 white for each block.

Join the squares with 1/4-inch seams in this way (B), producing a block 8½ × 8½ inches. Arrange the 4 blocks in this shape (C). Sew blocks together with 1/4-inch seams.

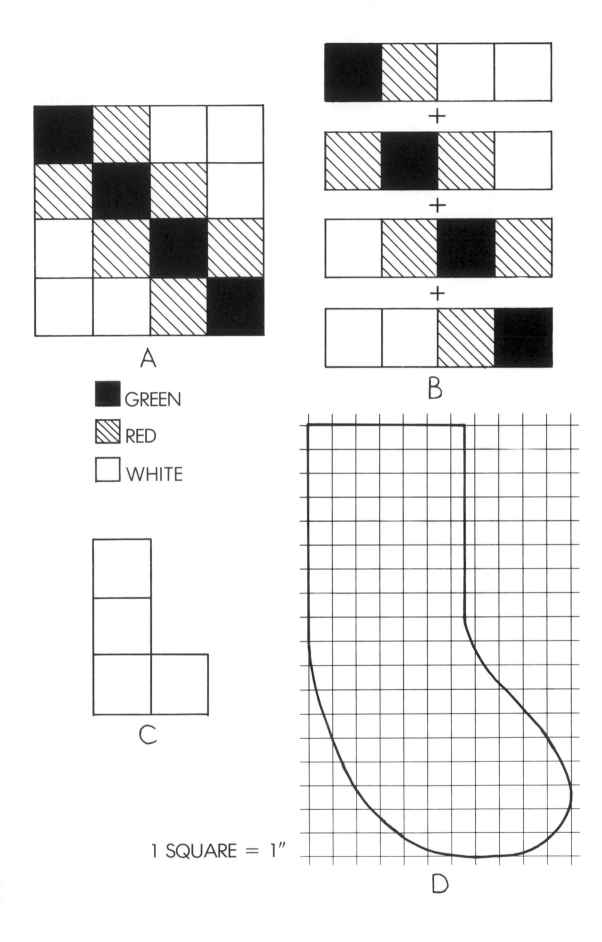

A

■ GREEN
▨ RED
☐ WHITE

B

+

+

+

C

1 SQUARE = 1"

D

123

Prepare front for quilting by cutting a rectangle of muslin 20 × 16 inches and a piece of batting. Baste layers to back of patchwork blocks.

For the back of the stocking, cut 2 rectangles and a piece of batting 20 × 16 inches. With the batting between the 2 rectangles, baste the 3 layers together.

Quilt front and back pieces by hand or machine work in diagonal lines from corner to corner with the lines 1½ inches apart.

With the quilted material prepared, enlarge stocking pattern (D) until it measures about 18 inches long and 10 inches wide.

Cut out stocking front and back. Sew pieces together with ¼-inch seam, leaving top open.

Fold the narrow piece of ribbon in half, forming a loop. Sew to edge with loop falling along back seam.

To finish upper edge, cut strip of muslin 3 × 13 inches for facing. With right sides together, sew facing to top. Press along seam line and turn facing to wrong side after joining ends. Sew lower edge to stocking with catch stitches.

Decorate the top of stocking with ribbon and lace. Start about 8 inches from one end to sew lace to one edge for about 20 inches. Repeat this procedure on other side of ribbon. Sew trimming to stocking 1 inch from top. Tie ends of ribbon into a bow.

Medallion Accent

The medallion creates a striking motif, giving a quilted design a different look. The design is built of triangles and rectangles around a center square, using a variety of solid and printed fabrics. It allows for a creative, carefree type of quilting reminiscent of the impressive Amish patterns. You can watch it grow to your own specifications. This piece can be used in various ways. It might hang on a wall, top a skirted table, or just add a decorative touch to an uninteresting spot.

Information to Note

Size: 28 × 28 inches

Materials: 1 yard patterned fabric from which center square, bands, and borders can be cut; try to find one that is comprised of different details 1½ yard solid fabric in a blending color from which triangles and backing can be cut
1 yard cotton flannel, to give the piece a flat look
Thread, in a blending color

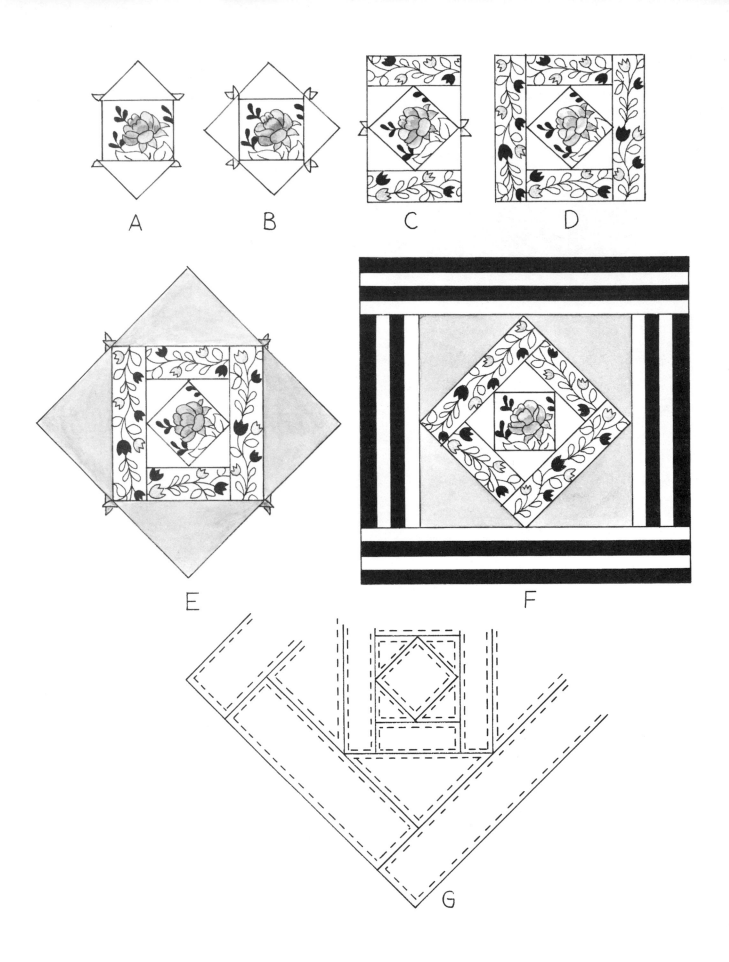

A

B

C

D

E

F

G

126

Directions to Follow

After studying the fabric carefully, decide where the pieces should be cut in order to create a pleasing effect. You will need:

> 1 square for center 6½ inches × 6½ inches
> 2 squares 5 × 5 inches for 4 triangles
> 2 strips 9 × 2 inches
> 2 strips 11 × 2 inches
> 2 squares 8½ × 8½ inches to make 4 triangles
> 2 strips 6½ × 17½ inches for border
> 2 strips 6½ × 28 inches for border

Cut a square of flannel 28 × 28 inches for filler.

Cut a square of backing material 30 × 30 inches.

With the parts cut, start to assemble them. Follow the diagrams shown here. Sew the parts together, using ¼-inch seam, with the right sides together.

Start by joining 2 triangles to opposite sides of the square (A). Notice that little "ears" seem to stick out beyond the square. Press the seams flat and cut off the little "ears."

Add triangles to other 2 sides of square (B).

Add 2 short strips (C) to opposite sides of the square. Follow with strips on other sides (D). Continue this way, adding the 4 triangles (E) and finally the border strips (F).

When the square is completed, press the piece flat.

Pin the flannel filling to the back of the top. Place this piece on the backing square, leaving a 1-inch extension along all edges. Baste the layers together.

Fold the backing over the top, making a ½-inch edging that resembles a binding. Slip-stitch in place.

To finish, outline each part with quilting stitches placed ¼ inch from each side of the seam line (G).

Comfy Throw

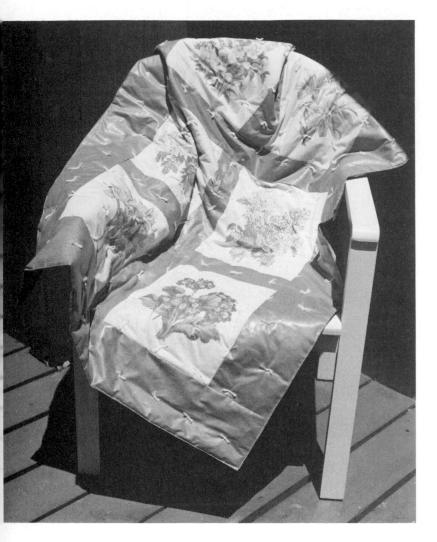

Having something pretty to toss over yourself when you need a moment of rest adds to the relaxing effect. This small version of a comforter is light in weight and made with a quiltlike construction. Instead of holding the layers together with quilting stitches, they are tied with knots. This makes the throw easier and quicker to construct, and at the same time the tiny tufts add a decorative touch.

Information to Note

Size: About 33 × 50 inches

Materials: 3 yards chintz in solid color

1 yard floral chintz. However, before buying remember that the amount depends on the size and arrangement of the design. Materials other than chintz can be used. Napkins were employed for this throw

Batting

Thread in a matching color

Ball of yarn in appropriate color for tying

Directions to Follow

To make the back, cut piece of fabric 34 × 51 inches. On the right side, place a series of dots using the design shown here. The marks are 3 inches apart (A).

Cut a piece of batting 33 × 50 inches.

Place batting on wrong side of backing and baste. Fold raw edge of backing over batting and baste.

To make the top, cut 6 floral blocks 11 × 9½ inches. For the setting you will need a strip 4 × 84 inches and a wider one for the border 6 × 102 inches.

After planning the floral arrangement, join 2 blocks with a vertical strip, using ½-inch seams. Repeat this procedure to make 2 other panels. Sew the horizontal panels together following the setting shown here (B).

To this section, sew side or vertical border strips. Add upper and lower border strips.

Turn under raw edges ½ inch and baste.

Pin top to backing. Baste the 3 layers together, starting at the center and working toward corners and then to the side edges. Baste outer folded edges together. Stitch along edge.

To tie the throw, use a short piece of yarn to make a double knot at each of the dots marked on the back. Take a straight ¼-inch stitch through the layers. Tie the yarn into a firm double knot. Cut the yarn, leaving ½-inch ends. After all the knots have been made, trim so they are all the same length.

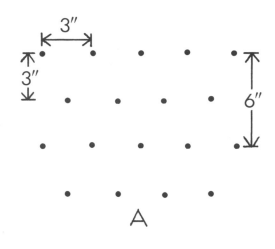

A

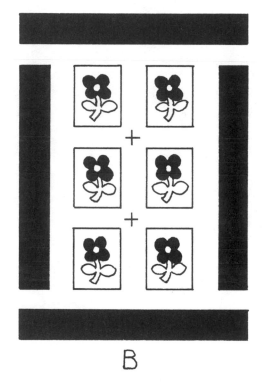

B

Pillow with a Patchwork Touch

Adding a patchwork appliqué to a plain pillow covering makes it decorative and pretty. Using a popular patchwork design, scraps of fabric can be used most effectively. This motif has many names, from Geese in Flight to Pinwheel.

Information to Note

Size: 17 × 17 inches

Materials: ¾ yard fabric for pillow covering in desired color—brown was used for this cushion
⅛ yard plain fabric in a neutral color for patch square
Scraps of material with tiny print. As many different ones as you wish can be used. Five were employed for this design, arranging them in an attractive sequence, which was repeated
Thread matching cover fabric and blending with patch fabric
Pillow form 16 × 16 inches

Directions to Follow

To make the patchwork block, make template 3 × 3 inches. Use this to cut out 8 plain squares and 8 of the different prints. If you use 5 prints, then cut 2 squares of each.

Cut diagonally across squares so you have 16 plain triangles and 16 printed ones (A).

Assemble 16 small squares, using 1 plain and 1 print triangle. Sew together with a ¼-inch seam (B).

Join the squares to form a 16-patch block. Assembling them in stripes makes the sewing easier and quicker (C).

When the block is completed, fold under the outer edges and baste in place.

To make the pillow covering, cut a square 19 × 19 inches for front and 2 rectangles—one 19 × 15 inches, the other 19 × 13 inches—for back.

Begin by appliquéing patchwork block to front square. Center it carefully on the right side and baste. Sew it securely around the edges by hand, using slip stitches, or by machine, stitching along the edge.

Make a hem along one of the longer edges in each rectangular piece, turn under the raw edge ½ inch and then 1 inch. Press and stitch.

With right sides together, place upper or smaller section on square, and then the lower or larger section. Baste parts together and stitch, making a ½-inch seam.

Turn to right side. Baste around the outer edge, being careful that the stitching line is exactly on the edge. Press.

Stitch 1 inch from edge. This produces a decorative fold around the pillow, which can now be inserted.

Slip pillow inside covering. Adjust fold so it stands up around the pillow.

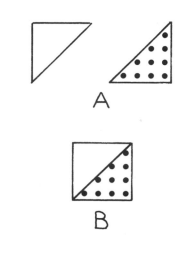

A

B

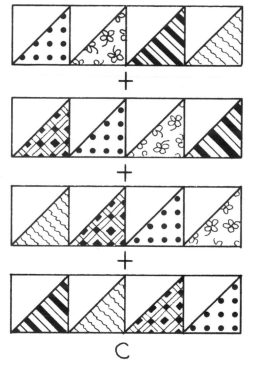

+

+

+

C

A Bag for the Walker

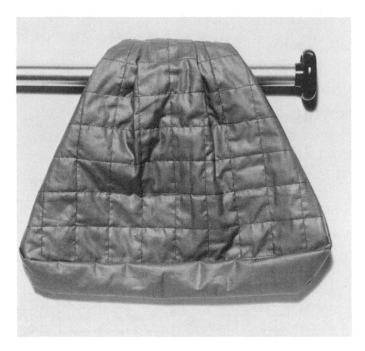

This quilted bag is both attractive and handy. It can swing jauntily on your arm as you stride up the avenue, or hang conveniently from the bar of a walker. Velcro closings make all of this possible.

Information to Note

Size: About 14 × 14 inches
Materials: For outside, 2/3 yard chintz or fabric of your choice; for lining, 2/3 yard in a contrasting print; for filler, 1/2 yard cotton flannel

1 spool thread in matching color
6 inches Velcro
Tools: Paper, pencil, and ruler for enlarging pattern shown here; needle, thimble, scissors, sewing machine and iron (the quilting can be done by hand)

Directions to Follow

Begin by enlarging pattern, to scale shown on diagram. Cut 2 pieces of chintz 16 × 14 inches and 2 pieces of cotton flannel. Draw quilting lines on flannel, 1½ inches apart unless you are using a quilting attachment on your machine.

Assemble material to be quilted by placing a piece of flannel on the wrong side of a piece of the outer piece. Baste together. Stitch on lines.

From these 2 pieces, cut front and back of bag. Also cut a strip of fabric using the longer pattern piece (26½ × 4 inches), and 1 of flannel. Also cut 2 small pieces (3 × 4½ inches) for extensions. Using these pattern pieces, cut out lining.

Mark center point on lower edge of larger sides and on both sides of band.

Stitch small pieces to ends of band, pleating the band ends to fit extension ends. Use ¼-inch seams. Pin band to quilted pieces at center points, right sides together. Stitch, using a ¼-inch seam. Press seams open.

Fold under the raw edges ¼ inch along top, sides, and extension ends. Stitch close to edge. Press.

Make a 1½-inch box pleat at top, reducing length to about 3 inches.

Construct lining. Fold under raw edges and press.

Put lining into bag, wrong sides together. Slip-stitch lining to bag.

Cut 2 strips of Velcro to fit upper edge of bag. Stitch 1 strip to under side of front piece and top side of the front following directions on package. Close, making handle.

Also sew Velcro to ends of band. Tuck inside and close.

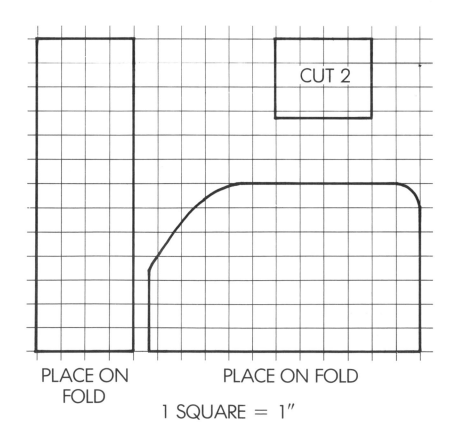

PLACE ON FOLD   PLACE ON FOLD

CUT 2

1 SQUARE = 1"

133

PART IV

Decorative Stitching

Suggestions

When you crochet, knit, and quilt, a piece of material results, but when you embroider, you embellish the fabric with a decorative touch. Embroidery is considered one of our oldest and loveliest art forms. Through the years it has changed just as fashions do. Today simple outline and cross as well as a variety of needlepoint stitches are in fashion. In case you have never embroidered, here are a few tips that will help you make the stitches suggested on the following pages.

Handling Needle and Thread

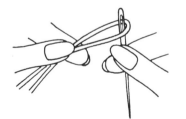

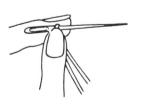

Threading. This isn't always as easy as it seems, especially when working with a heavy thread or yarn. Cut an 18-inch length from the spool or skein. Thread the needle with the cut end. A special threader will help, or you can try this procedure. Place the yarn around the eye of the needle. Grasp it firmly, close to the needle. Remove the needle. Continue to pinch the yarn to flatten it. Bring the eye of the needle down over the folded yarn a short way before releasing it. Be sure all of the yarn passes through the eye.

Holding the Needle. Grasp it between the thumb and first finger. It should touch the tip of the middle finger, which should be wearing a thimble. It is easier to pass the needle through the fabric if one is wearing a thimble.

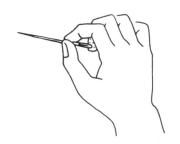

Starting a Stitch. Usually embroidery stitches are worked from left to right, in contrast to sewing stitches. The beginning point should be concealed as much as possible. Two or 3 very small running stitches, made toward the spot where the embroidery stitch is to begin, work nicely (A). Anchor it with a tiny backstitch (B). Sometimes a small knot can be used if the back of the fabric will not be seen.

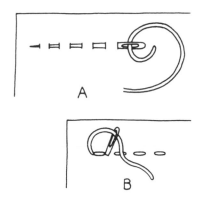

Ending a Stitch. The thread should be fastened inconspicuously on the wrong side. Running the needle under the last 2 or 3 stitches is one way to do it.

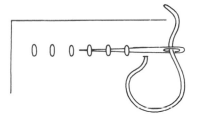

Beginning a New Thread. Introducing a new thread is often necessary. Again, it should be done so no one will notice it. Slide the needle under several stitches on the wrong side. This procedure will hold the new thread in place, especially if you use a backstitch through the last stitch. Then pass the needle to the right side of the fabric at the point where the next stitch is to be made.

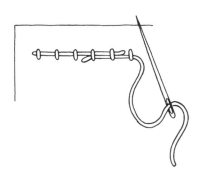

Stitches to Try

There are hundreds of embroidery stitches. However, if you analyze their structure, you realize that there are only 4 basic types: flat, such as cross and running; knotted, such as the French knot; linked, such the chain, and looped, such as blanket and feather stitches. Sometimes the types are combined to create interesting effects. On the following pages, you will find a few of these stitches.

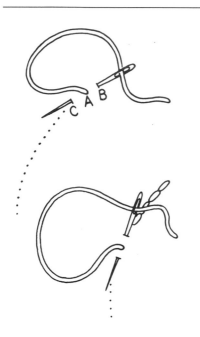

Backstitch. This is a versatile sewing stitch that resembles machine stitching when the stitches are the same length and even. It can be used effectively to embroider lines and outline a motif. Begin at the right-hand end of the line. Bring the needle to the right side, a stitch length from the starting point (A). Insert the needle at the end (B), bringing it to the surface a stitch length beyond (C). Let it reenter the fabric at A. Continue to work this way.

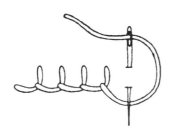

Blanket Stitch. Looping the stitch gives it a pretty as well as useful effect. It can decorate as well as hold down an edge. Working from left to right and between 2 guidelines, pass the needle to the right side on the lower line. Hold the thread in place with the left thumb. Insert the needle a short distance to the right at the upper guideline. Let it reappear directly below in the lower guideline and inside the loop. Pull the thread through the loop. Continue to make the stitches this way.

Chain Stitch. This stitch can be used in a row or separately to form a floral motif, as in the Lazy Daisy Stitch. Begin by bringing the needle to the right side of the material. Hold the thread down with the left thumb, forming a loop, as you return the needle to the fabric at A. Let it reappear a short distance below at B. Draw the thread through the loop, but leave it loose. For the next stitch, insert the needle inside the loop at point B. Try to keep the loops evenly spaced.

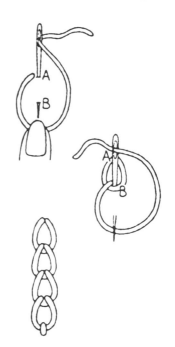

Cross-Stitch. Easy-to-do makes this one of the more popular stitches. The regularity of the length and the slant of the stitches is most important in order to create a pretty effect. The design can be stamped directly on the fabric or made by counting threads on even-weave fabric or with double-thread canvas, as well as working on gingham.

Instead of embroidering 1 cross-stitch at a time, the effect seems better if 2 separate rows of single slanting stitches are made, the second crossing the first. Start at the lower right-hand corner of the line, bringing up the thread at A. Insert the needle diagonally above at B. Let it come up directly below at C. Work with the needle in a vertical direction.

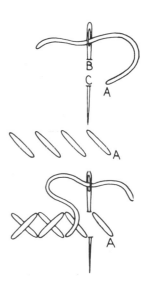

Feather Stitch. This decorative stitch is worked like a blanket stitch. The stitches, however, are made on an angle, creating a zigzag effect. Two guidelines will help to keep the

139

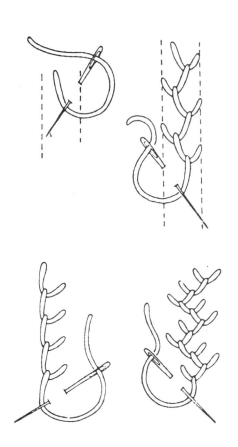

stitches evenly placed. Bring the needle to the surface at the top of the line to be covered. Hold down the thread with the left thumb. Take a diagonal stitch to the right slightly below the starting point. Draw the needle through the loop and over the working thread.

Loop the thread to the left-hand side for the second stitch. Slip the needle diagonally under the material. Point it toward the design line and pull it through as you did for the first stitch. Continue to alternate the stitches from right to left. Be careful to keep the stitches the same in size and an equal distance from the design line.

Variations of the feather stitch are also attractive. Two versions—the single and double feather stitch—are shown here.

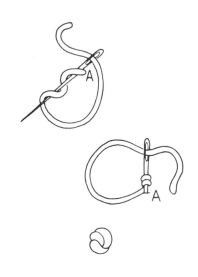

French Knot. Thread is twisted around the needle to create beadlike dots. The three-dimensional effect is most pleasing as a filling in a small area. The size of the knot can vary depending on the weight of the yarn and the number of twists. However, the attractiveness of the knot depends on the tautness of the thread around the needle. You will be more successful if the needle is large enough to let the thread to be pulled easily through the wound thread and, at the same time, maintain its firmness.

Let the needle come to the surface at the point where the knot is to be made (A). Grasp the thread firmly between the left thumb and first finger quite close to the fabric. Keeping the thread taut, twist the thread around the needle. Insert the needle close to the point where the needle emerged. Pull the needle through the coiled thread to the underside.

Herringbone Stitch. This is another stitch that requires a definite regularity in the slant and spacing of the stitches. Working from left to right, between 2 guidelines, will promote this effect.

If you study the diagram shown here, you will notice that the needle emerges on the lower line (A) and reenters the fabric at B, making a diagonal stitch. It emerges again to the left at C, a short distance from B. With the thread carried over the first stitch, insert the needle at D, and let it emerge at E to begin the third diagonal stitch. Observe that ends B and C on the upper line are centered between points A and D on the lower line. Continue to make the following stitches in the same way. When the stitches are completed they can be laced, threaded, and tied to create many different looks.

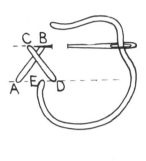

Outline Stitch. When a solid line is needed, this is a stitch to use. In appearance, it is similar to a *Stem Stitch.* However, the position of the thread is held above the line, whereas it is below for the Stem Stitch. Both stitches are made from left to right.

For the Outline Stitch, bring up the needle at the end of the line to be followed. Insert it a short distance to the right, letting it emerge halfway between these 2 points.

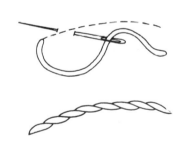

Satin Stitch. The stitch is used for a solid effect. The straight flat stitches are placed close together. Work between two guidelines. Bring up the needle in the left-hand guideline (A). Insert the needle in the right-hand line (B) letting it emerge just below (A) at (C).

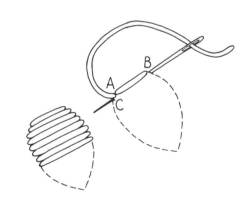

141

Tent Stitch. This is the basic stitch used for needlepoint. It can be worked in various directions—horizontally, vertically, and diagonally. When the stitches are made in a horizontal or vertical direction, the stitch is also called the Continental Stitch; diagonally, it is called the Basketweave Stitch. Working with a frame or hoop will help to keep the canvas from being pulled out of shape.

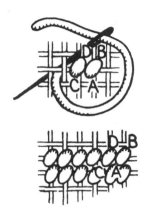

Horizontally. Begin by bringing up the needle at the lower right-hand side of the area to be covered (A). Let the needle reenter at B, making a diagonal stitch, 1 thread to the right and 1 above. To construct the second stitch, come up at C, 2 threads to the left and on a line with A. Insert the needle at D. Continue across the row, working from right to left. At the end of the row, turn the canvas. Make an identical row of stitches, using the same holes as in the first row. Because the canvas is turned, all stitches are made from right to left.

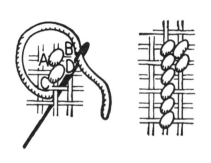

Vertically. Work from top to bottom. Begin at the upper point. Let the needle emerge at A. Insert it at B, 1 thread to the right and 1 above. Come up at C, 2 threads below and 1 to the left. Reenter the canvas at D, 1 thread to the right of A and below B. Proceed to end of row. Turn the work so the stitches can be made from the upper to the bottom edge.

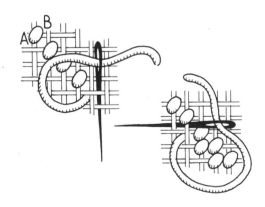

Diagonally. The stitches are worked in two directions—first downward with the needle in a vertical position, and then upward with the needle held horizontally.

Start at the upper point and work downward. Make a diagonal stitch over 1 intersection of canvas (A–B). Then slip the needle vertically under the canvas, appearing 2 threads below.

142

Begin the second row, working upward. Make the stitches to the left of the first row. Take a small stitch over a single intersection of canvas, putting it in a space left by the first row. Slip the needle horizontally under 2 vertical threads of canvas ready to take the next stitch. Proceed this way, working first from top to bottom, and then from bottom to top.

Tramé Stitch. To give canvas stitches a raised look, a long stitch is used as a padding. It stretches over a pair of double canvas threads, forming a line to be covered. It should be concealed by tent stitches.

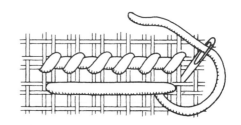

Supplies and Tools

There should be a compatability between the fabric, thread, and equipment if the finished work is to be beautiful. The stitch should seem right for the material and the thread right for the stitch. Keeping a record of successful stitch interpretations will make embroidering more pleasurable.

Fabric. Most material can be used as a background for embroidery. The one you select will probably depend on the fashion of the moment. It can vary from organdy, to homespun, to denim. For some, linen has been the favorite. However, whichever fabric you select, be sure it is woven on grain. This allows you to keep the rows of stitches evenly spaced and perfectly aligned.

Special *even-weave* fabrics are woven with heavier yarns, making it easy to count the threads. The threads form a natural grid over which cross-stitches can be made. The fabric is available in different-size grids. *Gingham* is another material that provides a good background for cross-stitching. Instead of counting threads, you count squares.

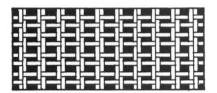

Canvas. Although there is a heavy fabric canvas, the one used for needlepoint has an open weave. It forms the foundation for the stitches. Canvas is made in 2 basic types: single-thread, or mono; and double-thread, or Penelope. Each is available in various sizes and fibers. The single-thread canvas seems easier to work on. In recent years, a plastic form has been widely used for appropriate items, where firmness is desired.

Hoops and Frames. Either of these pieces of equipment should be used. They are a definite aid in keeping the stitches even and the fabric smooth and flat. They are available in a variety of sizes and shapes. Always select one that allows you to work nicely. With a hoop, put the fabric over the smaller ring. Press the other ring over it. The fabric should be taut and the lengthwise and crosswise threads in perfect alignment.

Magnifying Glass. There is no need for you to squint or strain your eyes when doing needlework. A special glass to hang around your neck will correct the situation. It may take a little time to get accustomed to it, but you will enjoy using it eventually and be very pleased with your work.

Needles. Different types of needles are needed for different fabrics and kinds of embroidery. A needle with a sharp point, such as the crewel, works well on fabric. A blunt or tapestry needle performs better on canvas and even-weave fabrics. The popular crewel needle is short and has a long, slender eye. To enable the thread to pass through the fabric easily, select a needle that is slightly thicker at the eye end than the thread.

Scissors. Two pairs of scissors are convenient to have. A small pair, about 3 inches in length, is handy to snip threads, and a larger pair, about 4 or 5 inches long, will cut fabric. Both should have sharp points and narrow blades.

Thimble. If you really want to make beautiful embroidery stitches you must wear a thimble. It should be light in weight, fitting the middle finger comfortably.

Thread and Yarn. The type you select depends on the embroidery you are doing. Different types of thread can produce different effects when making the same stitch. Pearl cotton and 6-strand floss are commonly used. There are various yarns that vary from the very fine French wool to heavy rug-weight.

A Touch of Embroidery

If you have always wanted to be an artist but with no success, then try embroidering. It allows you to produce with thread what an artist does with paint. Combining glorious colors and fascinating forms can be most satisfying. On the following pages some ideas for using decorative stitches in a variety of ways are shown. If you wish, you can give each a personal touch by substituting your own choice of color and thread.

Crazy Quilt Picture

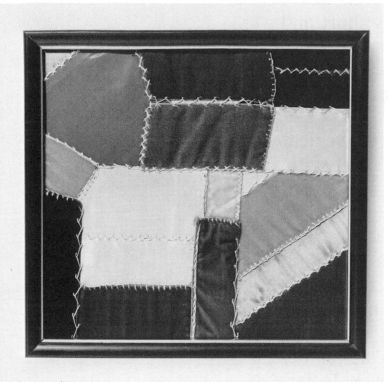

To have a piece of crazy quilting on your wall can be a conversation piece. Many people use a bit of an old quilt for this purpose. Crazy quilting always seems so colorful and luxurious with its velvets and satins embellished with embroidery, and fortunately this type of quilting can be relaxing to do. You don't have to be precise with the piecing. Instead, you can scatter the pieces at random, surprising yourself with the results. Although a suggested layout is shown here, you can rearrange the pieces to produce your own block. Of course, a quilt will be the result if you make more and more blocks.

Information to Note

Size: Finished picture 9½ × 9½ inches

Materials: Ribbons of velvet, satin, and taffeta in widths of 1, 1½, 2 and 4 inches. They can be new or old—from a corsage, a box of candy, a lovely gift wrapping, bringing a little nostalgia to the quilting as the antique quilts do. The colors range from dark to light blue, dark red to pink, dark green to chartreuse, and a neutral beige. The measurements on the chart indicate the approximate size of the 16 pieces. Cut the pieces as you quilt
1 spool thread in a blending color
1 skein 6-strand floss in neutral gold
⅓ yard muslin for backing
1 old-fashioned frame

Tools: The block can be made by hand or machine, using needles, thimble, scissors, hoop, and perhaps a sewing machine

Directions to Follow

Cut a square of backing material 11½ × 11½ inches. On it draw a square 10½ × 10½ inches. The piecing will cover this area. When ribbon is used, the edges can be sewn flat to the backing.

But if you use fabric, allow for ¼-inch seam allowances. Place the right sides of 2 pieces together and sew a ¼-inch seam. Separate the 2 pieces. Smooth it out over the backing. Pin in place so it won't move as the next piece is attached. Continue to assemble the pieces this way until the square is covered.

Add the embroidery. Select stitches that can span both sides of the seam line, such as blanket, feather, and herringbone. Other stitches can be used to give the square a more decorative look.

Frame it in a Victorian-type frame, and you may have created an heirloom-to-be.

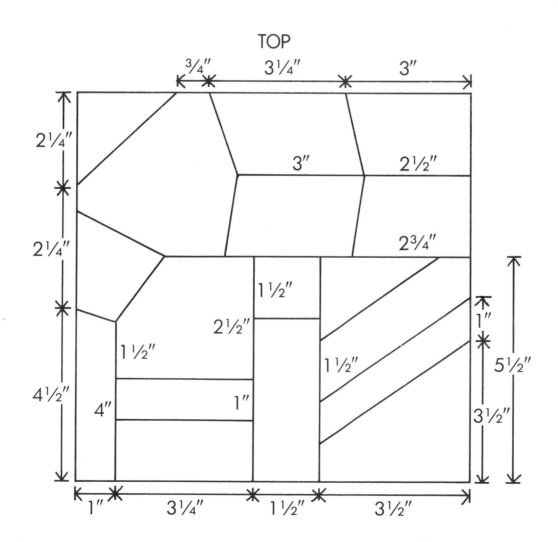

Bedside Caddy with Candlewicking

The clutter of a bedside table can be diminished by using a caddy tucked between the mattress and box springs. With its 4 pockets, there is a place within easy reach for glasses, magazine, tissue, and remote control. This one is not only practical but also pretty.

Information to Note

Size: Approximately 13½ × 15½ inches

Materials: 1 yard unbleached muslin
½ yard cotton flannel
1¾ yards gathered 1-inch ecru lace
1 skein 6-strand floss in desired color
1 spool white thread

Tools: Needles, thimble, pins, scissors, hoop, and sewing machine, plus ruler, tracing paper, pen, and iron

Directions to Follow

For back, cut 2 pieces 16 × 14 inches.

For pockets, cut 2 pieces 8 × 14 inches and 2 pieces 6 × 14 inches. Mark centers from upper to lower edges of each piece.

Enlarge design shown here until it measures about 2 inches. Transfer it to the center of smaller pocket, as shown. To make smaller pocket, pin cotton flannel to wrong side of front. Then add back section, right sides together. Stitch a 1/4-inch seam along 1 longer edge. Press. Turn back to underside and baste.

Candlewick the design, placing a French knot at each dot. Make the dots through the 3 thicknesses.

For other pocket, join 2 pieces, right sides together, along one longer edge. Turn and press. Finish both sections by stitching 1/4 inch from edge.

Pin first the larger and then the smaller pockets to the back along lower edge and sides. Baste. Also baste along center marking.

Baste lace to outer edges so the outside of the lace is inside. Place back section on top. Stitch around edges, making a 1/4-inch seam and leaving an opening at lower edge for turning.

Turn and baste around edge. Then stitch 1/4 inch around caddy and along center marking of pocket sections.

Cute Bib

A practical but interesting bib can be useful. It not only can stimulate an appetite, but also encourage good eating habits. Interpreting words and motif is easy to do when using outline and cross-stitches.

Information to Note

Size: About 13 × 9½ inches

Materials: ½ yard blue-and-white (or color of your choice) gingham, checks about 6 to the inch; be sure fabric is woven on grain so the rows of stitches will remain straight

Batting piece 13½ × 10 inches

1 skein red floss for the bear; 1 navy blue for the words

1 spool white thread

1 circle (2 parts) Velcro about ¾ inch wide

Tools: Graph paper (6 squares to an inch), tracing paper or marking pen, ruler, needles, pins, scissors, iron, and sewing machine

Directions to Follow

Enlarge pattern to the above measurements, the words so the tallest measures 1 inch and the overall length 6¼ inches, the bear 3¼ × 2½ inches.

Cut a piece of gingham 15 × 15 inches. On it trace the outline of the bib and then the words. Put the square in the hoop and begin the embroidery. Work with 3 strands of floss to do the words in outline stitch and then the bear in cross-stitch. Count the squares carefully as you do the cross-stitches.

With the embroidery completed, cut out the bib, leaving a ¼-inch seam allowance around the outline. Cut another bib for the underside. Place batting on wrong side of embroidered front, and pin. Seam back to front, right sides together, with a ¼-inch seam. Leave a small opening for turning. Press along stitching line. Turn and baste around edge. Press lightly. Slip-stitch opening to close.

Sew tabs of Velcro to back tabs, one to the underside, the other to the top side.

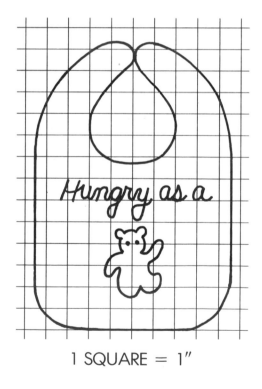

1 SQUARE = 1"

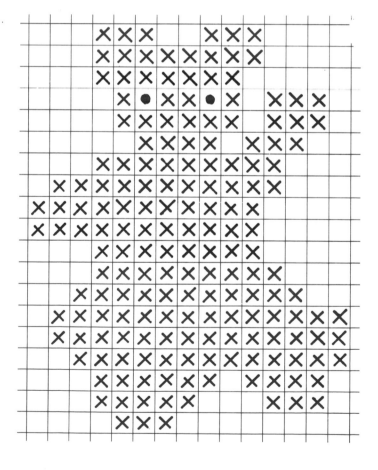

151

Poppy Pillow

If you need something to add a cheery note to the decor of one of your rooms, you might think about this pillow. It most certainly will add a striking accent. Using cross-stitches on even-weave fabric makes it easy to do.

Information to Note

Size: 11½ × 11½ inches

Materials: 1 package or ⅓ yard Aida or even-weave fabric
⅓ yard broadcloth for back of pillow
⅓ yard of unbleached muslin for pillow form
Roll of batting for filling
1 spool matching thread
1 skein red 2-ply sport yarn, some green for the leaves and black for center (the yarn gives a slightly fuzzy look; however, work with 6-strand floss if you wish)

Tools: Tapestry needle, hoops, scissors, ruler, transfer paper, marking pencil or pen

Directions to Follow

Increase the size of the design shown here until it measures 12 × 12 inches.

Cut a square of the even-weave fabric. Using pattern, transfer design to fabric. Cut yarn into 18-inch lengths, using red for the flower, green for the leaves, black for the center.

Put fabric in hoop. Fill in flower with cross-stitches, proceeding from right to left and then returning from left to right. Embroider the leaves, neck, and finally center.

When it is completed, remove from hoop. If necessary, press lightly with the right side down on a padded board.

To make pillow, cut square for back. Place right sides together. Stitch a 1/4-inch seam along the edges, leaving an opening on the lower side for turning. Press along stitching line. Turn inside out and press along edge.

Insert pillow, which you have made by stitching the 2 unbleached muslin squares together and stuffing it with batting. Close opening with slip stitches.

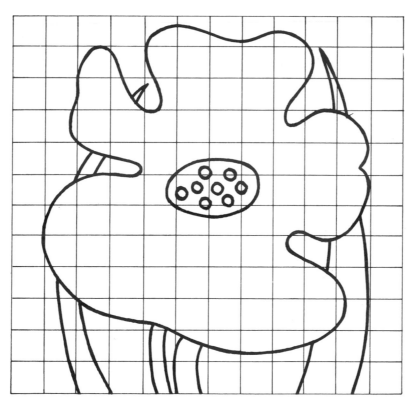

1 SQUARE = 1"

153

Bookmark with a Message

In the Victorian period, bookmarks were often embroidered and carried a message such as "Remember me." Today we are told to laugh or smile. In case you forget, tuck this bookmark in the world-shattering book you are reading. Perhaps life won't seem so stressful if you do.

Information to Note

Size: 1½ × 10 inches, including fringed ends

Materials: ⅔ yard ribbon, 1½ inches wide, in a color of your choice
1 skein silvery-gray 6-strand floss

Piece of double-thread canvas 1½ × 10 inches
Square of muslin 15 × 15 inches
1 spool matching thread

Tools: Needle, thimble, scissors, hoop, sewing machine

Directions to Follow

Cut 2 pieces of ribbon 10 × 1½ inches and a strip of canvas the same size. Baste the canvas to one of the ribbons and then baste to muslin square. Put in hoop and begin to cross-stitch, counting the canvas threads and using design shown here. When the letters are completed, pull out the canvas threads. This is an easy way to cross-stitch without marking the fabric. Remove ribbon from muslin.

Fringe ends of ribbon pieces for ½ inch at both ends. Sew together by stitching along the side edges.

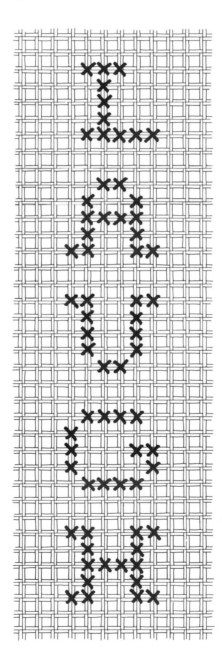

Mug Coasters

"Hi" has become such a popular greeting that it seems right for a "mug rug" to slip under that early cup of coffee. Made of plastic canvas, and embroidered in red and white, it seems to give a cheery feeling.

Information to Note

Size: 6 × 4 inches, including fringe

Materials: Piece of plastic canvas, 7 meshes to the inch, 4 × 4 inches, or 26 × 26 holes or squares (they seem easier to count than threads)
Small amount of worsted-weight yarn in a light color for the letters and a darker color for the background

Tools: Tapestry needle, scissors, ruler, paper clips or safety pins, and steel crochet hook No. 2 or 3.

Directions to Follow

Measure plastic carefully. Placing a dark sheet of paper under it will make it easier to count the squares. Mark the cutting lines with a bit of yarn, safety pins, or paper clips. Cut the square accurately. Round corners slightly.

Following the diagram, use vertical tent stitches to work the letters. Fill in background in the darker color, using horizontal tent stitches. Finish the top and lower edges with overcasting stitches, first to the right and then to the left. This produces a cross-stitch effect.

Add fringe to the side edges. Cut yarn into 2½-inch pieces. Insert hook in hole from right to wrong side. Pick up piece of yarn, which has been folded in half, and draw through hole. Put ends through loop and pull tight. Do this in each hole. When you have finished, check fringe for evenness. It should be 1 inch long.

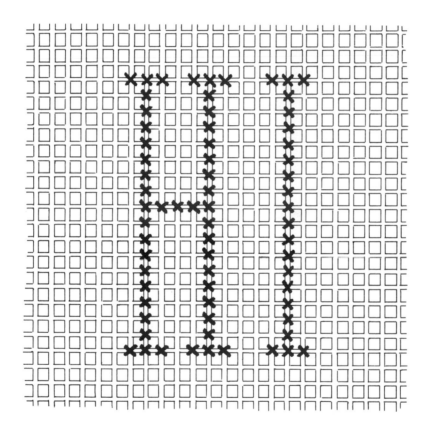

Silvery Tissue Box Cover

Have you ever noticed that there is always a box of tissue to be found in all types of rooms? Its use has become such a part of everyday living that it must be handy. Sometimes, however, the box seems wrong for the decor. It seems as if the box should not be obvious but instead blend into the background. This one is made of gray yarn, using a checkerboard stitch for a nice silvery effect.

Information to Note

Size: For a boutique box, 5½ × 4½ inches

Materials: 1 sheet 7-mesh plastic canvas (10⅜ × 13⅜ inches) 1 skein worsted-weight yarn in medium gray (of course, another color can be used if you wish)

Tools: Tapestry needle, scissors, paper clips

Directions to Follow

Cut canvas, 4 pieces each of 29 × 37 squares. If it is easier to count threads, count 30 × 38 threads.

Cut 1 piece of canvas for top, 29 × 29 square; 30 by 30 threads. Also cut opening in top 19 × 9 squares, 20 × 10 threads.

Following the diagram shown here, cover each side panel with a checker-board stitch. Frame these stitches with a border of tent stitches. Follow the chart for the top, using tent stitches and adding some cross-stitches as an accent. Overcast around edge of opening.

Join the various parts with overcasting stitches, first the sides and then the top to the sides. Overcast lower edge. Be sure that the edges are completely covered.

SIDE

TOP

159

Frame in Needlepoint

A special picture needs a special frame. To find the right one isn't always easy. The size and shape may be wrong and the cost too high. If this is the case, you could make a frame. This one is made of needlepoint, using a variegated yarn in tones of purple, soft blue, and green. An interesting pattern results that reminds one of lovely Far Eastern fabric.

Information to Note

Size: Outside 8 × 10 inches; inside, 5 × 7 inches

Materials: 15 × 15-inch square of single-thread canvas, 10 to the inch

1 ball variegated yarn such as Windrush by Yarns® Brunswick in colors of your choice—or try gray for a silvery effect

Batting the size of the frame

Lightweight nonwoven fusible interfacing

1 prepared soft frame mat board such as Yours Truly— or, using the pattern shown, you can cut a frame from cardboard.

Glue for fabric

Tools: Tapestry needle, masking tape, scissors, ruler, pencil or marking pen, X-acto knife if you are using cardboard

Directions to Follow

Enlarge frame pattern shown here to desired size. Cut square of canvas 15 × 15 inches. Transfer outline of frame to canvas. To remind yourself that you must cut the frame larger in order to turn edges under, mark a line 1 inch from the outline.

Bind edges of canvas with masking tape. Cut strands of yarn 18 inches long. Place canvas in hoop.

Begin to make tent stitches at lower right-hand corner and proceed in the usual manner. The variegated yarn will soon develop an interesting design. When the frame outline is completely filled, remove canvas from hoop. If the canvas seems out of shape, press gently, right side down on a padded surface, or block if necessary.

Use the directions that accompanied the mat boards for mounting the needlepoint and making the frame.

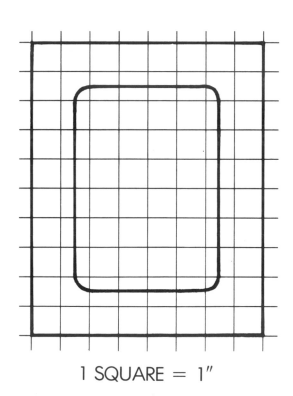

1 SQUARE = 1"

Belted in Spots

A belt has been a fashion item in recent years. When it is made with a leopard-skin motif, it becomes very special. Making it of needlepoint enhances its interest.

Information to Note

Size: The belt can be made in any length and in a 1½-inch width

Materials: Needlepoint canvas, 10 mesh to the inch
Tapestry yarn in dark brown and creamy beige
Grosgrain ribbon 1½ inches wide and required length, in dark brown or black
Thread to match ribbon
Buckle
Velcro

Tools: Tapestry and sewing needles, hoop, masking tape, pencil or marking pen, ruler, scissors

Directions to Follow

Before marking canvas decide how long the belt should be. Canvas does not have much "give," so measurement should be accurate. Remember to allow for the overlap and for sewing on the buckle.

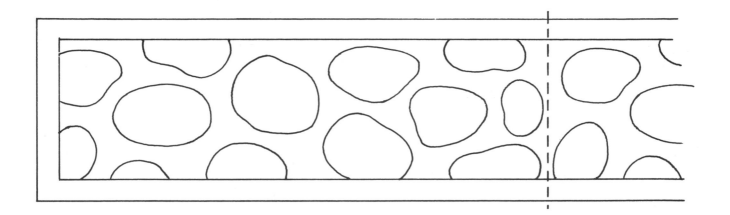

Enlarge pattern design shown here.

Mark canvas with the outline of the belt and the design. Notice that the pattern has been planned so it can be repeated as many times as possible. Try to use a piece of canvas wide enough so it can be placed in a hoop. Tape edges with masking tape.

Place canvas in hoop. Work design in tent stitches across the narrow portion. Work the spots, using the brown yarn, and then fill in the background with the beige.

When the needlepoint is completed, remove from hoop. Cut out belt, leaving a 1/2-inch margin for turning canvas edges under. Block if necessary.

Turn edges to wrong side 1/2 inch and baste. Cover edges with ribbon, turning under raw edges at ends. Hem to needlepoint.

Sew buckle to one end and a tab of Velcro a short distance away. Sew the matching tab to the underside of the other end, following the directions accompanying the Velcro.

Tulips for the Wall

Coats & Clark, Inc.

Tulips lend themselves nicely to a geometric floral design. This one made with needlepoint stitches is easy to make and most effective as a picture when hung. The design can also be used as a greeting card for a very special person.

Information to Note

Size: About 8 × 8 inches

Materials: 2 skeins No. 011, White; 1 skein each No. 821, Magenta; No. 510, Olive; and No. 958, Burnt Orange, of 3-ply Coats & Clark Red Heart® Persian-type needlepoint and crewel yarn,

Art. E. 28 Double-thread canvas, 10 holes to 1 inch, 8 × 8 inches Picture frame with backing board to fit

Tools: Tapestry needle, J & P Coats, No. 18; hoop; pen or marking pencil; ruler

Directions to Follow

Mark outline of picture on canvas. Indicate center of design with basting stitches, both lengthwise and crosswise. Commence the design centrally and work the given half following the diagram shown here and the colors indicated. Complete by working the other half to correspond. For a raised effect, use traméd tent stitches throughout. Each background square represents 1 canvas thread intersection or 1 stitch. The black arrows indicate the center and should coincide with the basting stitches.

When completed, block if necessary and frame.

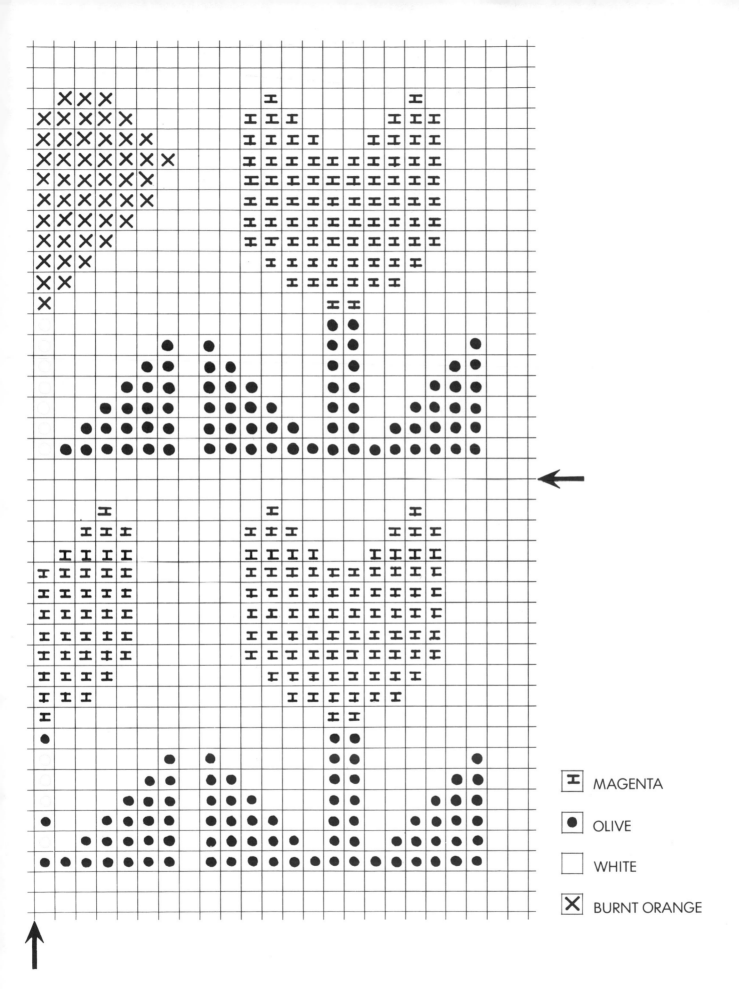

☐ MAGENTA

● OLIVE

☐ WHITE

☒ BURNT ORANGE

165

A Guide for Supplies

Sometimes it is difficult to find the right tool and material for certain types of needlework. If you have this trouble, you may want to contact a company mentioned here. Some provide a direct mail order service, whereas others will offer information or the name of a store near you. The variety of supplies carried by each company will differ.

American Needlewoman, 2946-50 S.E. Loop 820, Fort Worth, TX 76140, (800) 433-2231

Annie's Attic, 1 Annie Lane, Big Sandy, TX 75755-9401, (800) LV-ANNIE, *www.anniesattic.com*

Bucilla, 1 Oak Ridge Road, Hazelton, PA 18201-9764, (800) 233-3239, *www.bucilla.com*

Coats & Clark, Consumer Services, P.O. Box 12229, Greenville, SC 29616, (800) 648-1479, *www.coatsandclark.com*

Crystal Palace Yarns, 3006 San Pablo Avenue, Berkeley, CA 94702, (510) 548-9988

DMC, South Hackensack Avenue, Port Kearny Building, 10A, South Kearny, NJ 07032-4688, (800) 275-4117, *www.dmc-usa.com*

Halcyon Yarns, 12 School Street, Bath, ME, 04530, (800) 341-0282

Hearthside Quilts, 2048 Shelburne Road, Shelburne, VT 05482, (802) 985-8077

Herrschner's Inc., 2800 Hoover Road, Stevens Point, WI 54492, (800) 441-0838, *www.herrschners.com*

Home-Sew, 1825 W. Market Street, Bethlehem, PA 18018, (610) 867-3833

Kreinik Manufacturing, 3106 Timanus Lane, Suite #101, Baltimore, MD 21244, (800) 537-2166, *www.kreinik.com*

Lion Brand Yarn Company, 34 W. 15th Street, New York, NY 10011, (800) 258-YARN, *www.lionbrand.com*

Madeira USA Threads, 30 Bayside Court, P.O. Box #6068, Laconia, NH 03246, (800) 225-3001, *www.madeirausa.com*

Mary Maxim, P.O. Box 5019, 2001 Holland Avenue, Port Huron, MI 48061-5019, (800) 962-9504, *www.marymaxim.com*

National Association for Visually Handicapped, 22 W. 21st Street, NY, NY 10010, (212) 889-3141

Plymouth Yarn Company, Box 28, 500 Lafayette Street, Bristol, PA 19007, (800) 523-8932

Thumbelina Needlework Shop, P.O. Box 1065, Solvang, CA 93463, (805) 688-4136

Yarn Tree, P.O. Box 724, Ames, IA 50010, (800) 247-3952, *www.yarntree.com*

Other helpful websites that you might want to investigate are:

www.needlearts.com
www.crochet.about.com
www.crossstitch.about.com
www.needlepoint.about.com
www.knitting.about.com
www.woolworks.org
www.stitching.com
www.2busystitching.com
www.123stitch.com